AF612344

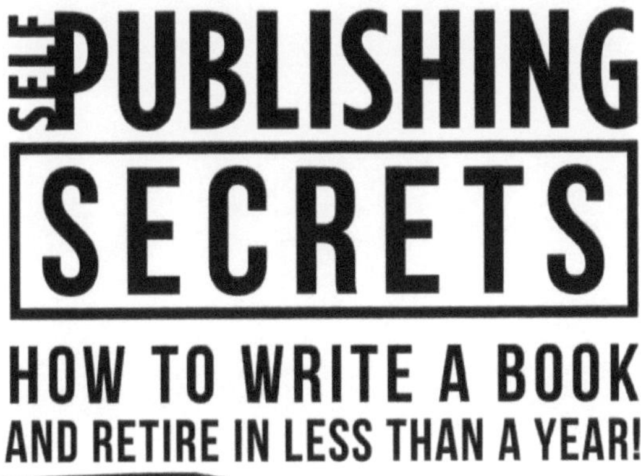

Kevin Albert

ISBN 978-9916-9940-4-7

Note: This work is derived from the author's experience in bookselling, writing, and publishing, and is meant to inform and inspire writers with tools and strategies for success in their own writing path. There is no single magic solution for everyone, and advice, wisdom, and insights should be carefully curated and adapted to suit each individual's needs, goals, and desires.

To my long *déjà vu*, Maia.

CONTENTS

SECTION 1: WRITE YOUR BOOK

SECTION 2: PUBLISH YOUR BOOK

SECTION 3: SELL YOUR BOOK

A gift just for you!

Would you like to **read my next book completely FREE**?
Scan the code below and **join my readers' club**!

Great surprises await you: be the first to read my new releases, listen to my audiobooks for free, get signed and personalized copies... and so much more!

WRITE YOUR BOOK

- A 7-STEP GUIDE TO WRITING A GOOD BOOK FAST -

You don't have to be great to start,
but you have to start to be great.

—ZIG ZIGLAR

Introduction

I remember one day, when I was seven or eight, my teacher gave me a note to give to my mother. The note asked my mother for a meeting so that they could talk about me and my academic performance (back in the days before teacher-parent WhatsApp groups). I don't remember exactly whether the meeting went well or not, but what I do remember is what my mother said when she got home: "Kevin, your teacher says you're a smart kid, but that she thinks you're writing badly on purpose to get her attention."

Sadly, I wasn't writing badly on purpose or to get attention; I simply wasn't very good at it, and my handwriting didn't help - and it still doesn't! To this day, I'm always being told I "write like a doctor".

Fear of writing is something that stayed with me right through my college years. My grades always got lowered in every test, either because I couldn't express myself well or because they couldn't read my handwriting. Unlike the rest of my classmates, I would cross my fingers for a quiz-type test, because I couldn't just write my way out of it.

Fortunately, my adventurous streak has always been stronger than my fears, and around 2012, I had the brainwave of turning a piece of college work I was doing for my MBA[1] into a book.

A book! Me?! What the hell was I thinking?

I could have spent the weekend cramming with three classmates and got an outstanding grade for that piece of work - but I decided to go it alone. I ended up spending **four years** on it.

I can promise you that the process wasn't easy; I came close to throwing in the towel on several occasions. Four years is a long time. Fortunately, I had a secret weapon: sheer stubbornness. When I set my mind to something, sooner or later, I do it. Armed with this tenacity that's always been a part of me, I overcame every obstacle that sprang up in my path, and - swearing to myself that I would never put myself through such an ordeal again - I found the way to finish my first book.

In mid-2016, everything was finally complete, and the long-awaited "publish on Amazon" button was finally ready for me to click.

Click!

So, what the hell happened after that moment that made me go from swearing I would never write another book, to making it

---

[1] Master of Business Administration

my life's work? And more importantly, how did I go from spending four years writing a book to finishing one in under 30 days?

That's exactly what this section is about:

1. I'm going to show you **the amazing things that await you after you publish your book** (things I could scarcely have imagined), so that you don't have to depend on pig-headedness, like I did.

2. I'm going to **teach you the exact system that enabled me to go from writing a book in four years to doing it in 30 days or less**, saving you years of learning and of trial and error.

And, best of all, you don't need:

To be a great writer.
To have a degree.
To be a bookworm.
To have a lot of free time.
To be an expert in your field.
...

All you need is something you want to tell the world. My mission is to show you how to do it.

Shall we get started?

CHAPTER 1

Why write a book?

(Step 1)

I bet, since you're reading this book, you think you already have this point covered and you can skip this chapter. Don't make that mistake; without a doubt, this is the most important chapter in the whole book.

Having a **just because** and having a **sufficiently important reason** can mean the difference between writing your book in 30 days, taking a really long time (like I did), or - most commonly - never finishing or even starting it.

Of course, not all books can be written in the same space of time; some good books are so specific and short that they can be written in one day (I know of more than one such book), while others are so long or require so much prior research that they can take several months. But it should never take **years**!

As I said, my big "mistake" - which made my first book *Branding Secrets*[2] take **much longer than it should have** to see the light of day - was not having a **sufficiently important** reason for it.

Branding Secrets began as a piece of work for a Corporate Image and Identity module on my Master's in Business Administration at college. Of course, within a traditional education system, your motive is clear: **passing**. No one was going to give me a prize for writing a book that was revolutionary in the branding world or one with the potential to change thousands or millions of people's lives. The only thing that mattered was that my teacher liked it, so that I could get a good grade. And I did. With only twenty written pages, my work was the only one to pass with honors, out of over forty students on that MBA course.

But once I had passed, what was my motive for continuing to write? As I'm sure you've figured out, I had none. So how did I manage to finish my book? That's easy: through willpower. The only source of energy I had at my disposal when it came to finishing my book was pure and simple pig-headedness. I can't think of any better recipe for ensuring a project's failure. Despite this, and against all odds, I managed to finish and publish my book - albeit four years later.

How much easier and faster would it have been to write if I had known what awaited me when it was finished? How long would I have taken to finish it had I known **the power a book has to change your life**?

---

[2] *soykevinalbert.com/books/bs*

What can a book do for you?

In a word: EVERYTHING.

Think I'm exaggerating? Or that that's just my opinion? Nope. **A book can fulfil your needs on every single level**.

But don't just take my word for it; I can prove it scientifically, using Maslow's hierarchy.

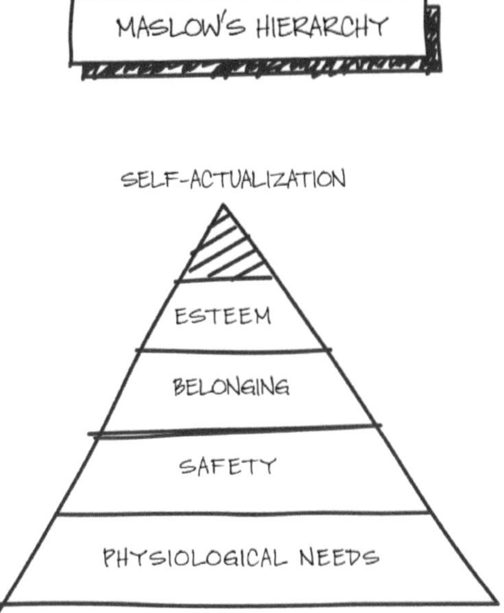

Maslow's hierarchy of needs is a motivational theory that aims to explain what drives our behavior by showing human needs ranked on a five-level pyramid.

This theory posits that as our more basic needs are fulfilled (the lower levels of the pyramid), humans develop more elevated needs and wants (the higher levels). However, usually, a book will fulfil the writer's needs in reverse order - that is, from top to bottom. Let's take a look.

1. The need for self-actualization.

Every writer I have spoken to, and every writer I've read about, agrees that finishing a book and holding the first hard copy of it in your hands produces a sensation of accomplishment and self-actualization that is hard to beat. It's not surprising, considering you have just achieved a feat that most people dream of but only 1% actually do. Don't deny yourself this extraordinary feeling of self-actualization.

2. Esteem needs.

Have you ever wondered why we need to be considered experts on certain topics? To have a college degree, maybe? Or two? Three? A masters? A blog? A YouTube channel? A gazillion Instagram followers?

Other than having a doctorate or being on a TV show, I can't think of a better way to achieve immediate recognition than by writing a book. But, unlike the doctorate, it won't take half your life to finish - especially if you follow the tips in this book.

3. Belonging needs.

Almost parallel to our need for esteem comes the need for belonging. Like it or not, writing a book will automatically make you a member of the select club of super-writers: one that, as I mentioned, only 1% of people are invited to join.

You know how sharing political views, a nationality or a football team brings people together? Well, wait till you experience the camaraderie produced by talking to other people who have been through the painstaking, solitary process of becoming a writer. It's like spending months lost in a country where you don't know anyone, and suddenly bumping into your oldest friend.

I can promise you that, in less than a year and requiring no further effort on your part, several very interesting people will have joined your circle of friends: people who, just like you, wrote a book.

4. Safety needs.

Do you think having a salaried job provides security? Wait till you experience the peace of mind of having a **recurring passive income**. It's like getting your pension ***now***, but without the uncertainty. In case you didn't know, experts agree that the days of pensions as we know them are numbered.

But don't panic; that's why you're here. You can tailor your own retirement plan - and not only that, but you can create as many **retirement books** or plans as you want.

If you're a clued-up person, then it's a very good idea for your retirement to depend on you and not on a tight-fisted, incompetent government.

5. Physiological needs.

Obviously, both the passive and non-passive (services, talks, and so on) incomes from your book will enable you to put food on the table and sleep easy at night: two very important basic physiological needs.

But there is a third need that writing a book can fulfil, and it's not such an obvious one: the need for reproduction.

Because whether you like it or not, writing a book will turn you into a much more interesting and attractive person. And in a society that claims to be sapiosexual[3], I think this is a much better alternative to salsa classes when it comes to finding a partner.

Okay, so now we've scientifically corroborated the fact that **a book has the power to fulfil all your needs**. But no matter how impressive this headline seems, or how nice it is to hold the

---

[3] By definition, a sapiosexual is someone who finds intelligence sexually attractive or arousing.

benefits of a book up alongside the pyramid of human needs, this may not be **enough motivation for you to ensure you both start *and finish* your book**, since you probably already had most of these needs covered.

So, if you want to find a source of motivation strong enough that it doesn't run out halfway through, you're going to need to be a lot more practical and pragmatic.

Why write a book?

There are as many reasons to as there are stars, so I'm just going to focus on what I think are **the 7 best reasons to write a book**:

1. Live without having to work.

Most of us spend our lives waiting for five o'clock so we can go home, waiting for Friday to start the weekend, waiting for August to go on vacation, waiting to turn sixty-seven so we can finally **retire and be free to do what we want**.

But be careful. Many of us may not make it to sixty-seven, or life expectancy may increase to the point that we're made to work five or ten years longer, or pensions may run out, or we may not have the good health to enjoy retirement, and so on. So why risk it? Why wait?

It's true that earning millions of dollars from a first book is a rare occurrence, and it depends on having - among other factors - exceptional talent and a considerable amount of luck.

But **earning a thousand dollars a month through passive income from your book requires nothing more than a good strategy**.

Of course, your first book might earn you a little (or a lot) more than that (although I can't guarantee it). You may also make less, or need twice or three times as much in order to retire the way that you want. No problem. All you have to do is write another book or two...or as many as you want!

2. Fire your boss.

Unlike the reason given above, this one isn't about no longer working, but no longer working for your dick of a boss - a highly motivational idea. In this case, your book wouldn't be your (main) source of income, but **the way you generate your income**.

Let's look at an extreme example. Let's say you decide to give your book away for free (I don't recommend it at first). Your income from sales of your book would be zero, but you would start to reach more people than if you were charging for it. These people would consider you an expert, and - if you did your homework - you'll become their preferred option when they need to hire an expert in the subject of your book.

Your book can be the best ad campaign for selling your products or services.

This is the most common situation. Even if you wrote a mediocre book and have no strategy, offers will start to pour in. The lives of many non-fiction writers change for the better, whether they planned it or not.

Bear in mind that being an "expert" is not an absolute. If you know just a little more than someone else on a given topic, to them, you are an expert.

Anyway, in your case - starting with a clear reason in mind for tailoring the best strategy for your specific situation - your life will not only change for the better, it will change in precisely the direction that you choose.

If you've just been cruising along, dictated by the circumstances and events of your day-to-day life, this could be a good moment to set a course you can sail toward.

Writing a book is a great opportunity to take the helm in your life.

3. Get your dream job.

In my dreams, I don't work, but I understand that many people need the approval and recognition that you can only get from X person or company considering them good enough to work for them. If this sounds like you, writing a book will multiply by one hundred (I made this statistic up, but I don't think I'm too far off) your chances of being the chosen candidate, even without an open selection process!

Yes, this means that if you write a book bearing in mind your aim to get a particular job, you can more or less publish it and then sit back and wait for that call - the company, and not you, will be able to decide you are the right person for the job. Have your conditions ready.

It might sound like I'm bragging, but it's really just common sense. If you write a book on a given subject, your target market is probably going to include the person hiring at the company (or company type) where you want to work. And if you write the book demonstrating you're an expert in the topic and dropping in the idea you're open to job offers (for example, in your LinkedIn profile), particularly that you're open to a challenge, which employers love, you have a great edge over people who may even be far more qualified than you.

A book is the best way for an "expert" to show off.

This doesn't mean that, if you're trying to find work, you can forget about actively looking for a job. All I want to do is highlight the competitive advantage a book can give you when it comes to being the winning candidate.

Now, all you have to do is plan out a good strategy to ensure your book ends up in the right hands.

4. Forget about your mortgage.

Maybe you're not looking to stop working; maybe your boss is great and you've already found your dream job. Maybe you already think your life is perfect just the way it is. But wouldn't it be a little more perfect if you could forget about your mortgage, change your car every two years instead of every twenty, or go on vacation more often to more exotic places?

It's up to you. Which expense sucks away a little of your happiness every month? What desire have you been postponing for years, waiting for a pay rise or a little lottery win?

The recurrent income from your book will enable you to improve your quality of life by several degrees. Bear in mind that as soon as you publish your book on Amazon (or anywhere else), you will receive a check or deposit every month from book sales - your royalties - without you having to lift a finger, and for the rest of your life[4]. Amazon will take care of absolutely everything, so all you will have to do is decide what to use your new "pay rise" for.

---

[4] No one knows if Amazon will be around forever, or if they will change their conditions without prior notice. Don't worry - there are a lot of ways to get by without Amazon. For the moment, your only goal - and the aim of this book - is to start and finish your book.

5. Spend your life traveling.

The vast majority of people, when you ask them what they would do if they won the lottery, don't miss a beat before replying "travel", "travel more", or "travel the world". Personally, I think this answer is just a knee-jerk reaction that reveals that that person has never truly stopped to think what they would really do if money were no object. Even my mother, who can't be out of the house for more than a few hours, gives the same answer. I don't know about that...

In any case, whether this is really your dream or you just want to try it for a while, writing a book can give you this power, too. You also have several options to see which best suits you and your specific situation:

a) Spend your life traveling without working:

   Traveling thanks to the passive income generated by your book or books.

b) Spend your life traveling while working:

   - Traveling thanks to the services you sell via your book. Your services should be available online, not just face-to-face.

   - Traveling thanks to the passive income generated by your book while you continue to create new books. If you can only offer your services face-to-face, you can make writing books your new job.

The best thing about this is that, if you really want, you can start virtually straight away. For example, if you don't mind starting out in, let's say, Thailand, all you need is around three hundred and fifty dollars a month in income - passive or otherwise - which is not too difficult to achieve.

You might fall in love with the country and decide to stay there forever, never needing to work again. You might get bitten by the travel bug and want to visit other countries (or improve your quality of life in the one you're in). Given that you will have a lot of free time, why not write another book? You could even write about your experience. Picture it: *How I Retired and Moved to Thailand After Writing my First Book.*

When you publish your new manuscript, you'll have double the passive income, if not more, since you will have learned a lot since you published your first.

Now that you've decided to double your pay, maybe you'll want to try living in Bali. I've heard it's amazing, and with a thousand dollars a month you can live like a king, all inclusive. And what about publishing another book after that? Where do you want to move to next? Sounds good, huh? Best of all, this is **more than feasible**.

Are you getting ready to throw yourself into this yet?

6. Be immortal.

I've always been fascinated by the concept of immortality. I was a big fan of the *Highlander* saga as a child, and nowadays it's *Black Mirror* episodes centered around the idea that captivate me. I even follow news on new technological and scientific discoveries that suggest that, in a not-so-distant future, we will be able to live forever. But until that happens (if it ever does), the best way of guaranteeing your immortality is to leave behind a legacy.

I'm sure you've heard the expression: "every man should plant a tree, have a child, and **write a book**." All three of these ideas revolve around leaving a legacy and becoming immortal.

They say that you only truly die when no one remembers you any more. Writing a book is a fantastic way to keep your memory alive forever, and - contrary to what I believed when I was little - it's much easier, faster and less effort than having a child :)

7. Change the world.

I decided to leave this reason for last, because it's "my" reason. This is my greatest source of energy, my raison d'être while writing these words.

Personality, I think you can measure a person's worth or greatness by the number of lives they touch or enrich. As a serial entrepreneur, every one of my many projects is conceived as a way to cover a need that people find unfulfilled.

The problem is that when your direct intervention is needed in order to change people's lives, your potential to change the world radically decreases. How many people can you offer your services to in one year? Ten? Fifty? A thousand?

Even in the highly unlikely event that you can touch a thousand people's lives in a year, it's still an insignificant number. Your potential is tremendously limited because you need to dedicate x minutes or hours to each person in order to bring about significant change in their lives; there are only twenty-four hours in a day, and you can't be in two places at once.

Or can you?

A book will enable you to "be in two places at once", exponentially increasing your ability to reach and touch the lives of millions of people anywhere around the world, with a product that's accessible on any size budget.

Do you have an important message to share? Something you believe we should all know? or do you "simply" know how to make the best vegan burgers in the entire world or know a trick for traveling on a shoestring?

Without a doubt, there are dozens of ways to expand your message and your knowledge beyond one-on-one: conferences, a blog, a YouTube channel, and more, and they are all perfectly valid. Even so, my advice is still to start with a book. This will open numerous doors for you, and your opportunities to keep spreading your message will increase - but first, you need to take that first step.

Are you ready to begin your first book?

CHAPTER 2

Excuses and writers' block: How to overcome them

(Step 2)

Now you're clear on your reason for doing this, write it down. Congratulations! You have just completed the most important step in the journey of every successful writer.

If your chosen reason is important enough, nothing can stand in the way of you finishing your book.

But let's imagine you only chose a good reason. Good reasons are all well and good, and they get you far out in front of people who just started writing one day because they suddenly felt like it, but they're not foolproof.

What's the difference between a good reason, and a sufficiently important one? Let's take a look at an example:

- **A good reason**: I would *like* to write a book so I can get a better job and feel more accomplished.

- **A sufficiently important reason**: I *have* to write a book if I want to safeguard my children's future[5].

Does this mean that if you only have a *good* reason, you will never finish your book? No - it just means that you're going to need to brace yourself for the dreaded **writers' block.** And believe me, it will hit you.

If your reason is not important enough, your excuses will be.

Have you ever signed up for the gym totally convinced that this time, you'll get your dream body or shift those few extra pounds? What happened to your motivation after a few short weeks? Your *one-time* energy - in other words, your *good* reason - clashed with your *long-lasting* excuses: "I don't think I'll go today; it's raining", "I had a shitty day today and I deserve a rest", "I had an awesome day today and I want to celebrate it", and so on.

As a personal trainer, one of the most important parts of my job is preparing my clients for these kinds of excuses, because they will crop up sooner or later. If you wait for them to happen before doing anything about them, it will be too late.

---

[5] This is the real reason of a client and friend of mine, who puts away a monthly portion of the proceeds from his book in an indexed fund (*soykevinalbert.com/indexa*). We calculated that, by the time his son is 22, the fund will be worth somewhere between $50,000 and $120,000.

Just like in fitness, excuses or writers' block always consist of the same thing - but don't worry, I have good news. There is an easy solution for them.

The 5 most common excuses writers make.

1. A book has to be perfect.

Without a doubt, this is my main block. I've always been a real perfectionist, so my projects have taken much longer than they should have. Of course, writing my first book was going to involve this, too.

I'm normally a perfectionist, even with the small tasks that have no real impact on my life, so imagine the unnecessary and inhuman effort I made when writing *Branding Secrets*. Of course, it was my first book and - I believed at the time, my last - and I thought it was going to be my legacy and show how good or mediocre I was, that people were going to judge me by it, and that once it had been published I could no longer change it.

My head was swimming with these thoughts and many others, and the same happens to lots of new writers. Well, let me tell you two things: firstly, most of them aren't true, and secondly (and more importantly) the success of a non-fiction book doesn't lie in how well-written it is, but in whether or not it delivers what it promises.

Unlike with fiction books, readers are not merely looking to be entertained or enjoy the pleasure of reading. When we buy a non-fiction book, we're looking to learn something, resolve a specific problem, acquire a new skill, and so on.

As such, even if your book isn't perfect - even if it's a total disaster in terms of spelling, grammar and structure - **if a reader finishes your book feeling that they found what they were looking for, you will have a satisfied reader**.

Does this mean I give you my blessing to write a pile of trash? Of course not! All I'm saying is that you should focus on fulfilling your promise, and this will help you overcome "analysis paralysis" or "perfectionists' block". There will be time to worry about form later.

Still unsure what I mean? Here are a few more tips to help you get past the blockage:

- What might be just a rough draft for you could be a finished book for someone else.

- Your book will go through at least one meticulous editing process before being published, so relax.

- When someone reads your book on Kindle, they have the option to let you know automatically if they come across an error; it's kind of like having a whole team of editors working for you. Not half bad, huh? But be careful - don't rely exclusively on readers.

- **On-demand printing from Amazon enables you to keep making corrections and improvements FOREVER.** Missed out an apostrophe? Had a reader point out a typo? Want to add additional information? No problem: you can edit the file, re-upload it and you're good to go. This is the beauty of this type of printing, among many other advantages.

Remember: perfect is the enemy of good.

2. You have to be an expert to write a book.

As we've already seen, you DON'T need to be an expert to write a book. You don't need a doctorate or to have read every single book, article and publication on a given topic. But...

Writing a book will turn you into an expert.

There's no better way to become an expert at something than to try and teach that something to someone else.

I have so many crazy examples of people I know doing this that I could write a whole book on them alone. I myself am an example of it; when I started writing *Branding Secrets*, I had a lot of experience and some very interesting things to say on the subject, but I was just a student back then and no one would have thought to ask me about branding. Now, I'm a major expert in low cost branding and I get offers from businesspeople and entrepreneurs from all over the world to help them with their brands, and they pay me very well for it (up to **a hundred times more** than in my old job working for other people). But, as I say, I did already know a lot about the topic. I was already an expert. My book really helped to give me more reach and visibility. So, to help you overcome your block, I'm going to tell you about one of those crazy examples I mentioned: one where the egg came before the chicken (or was it the other way around?). In other words, the book preceded the expert:

> After spending two years working as a physiotherapist, traveling the world aboard the biggest cruise ship from the *Royal Caribbean*, I decided to make the most of the sales expertise I had acquired over the course of all those months[6]. So, on my return to Spain, I applied to work as a salesman; it was the only work where I could make a living close to what I had been earning on the boat.

---

[6] In addition to my Physiotherapy qualifications, to work for many cruise companies you needed to spend several months at the company's Steiner facilities in the UK, where you think they're going to be teaching you new treatment techniques when what they're really doing is teaching you how to sell ice to an eskimo.

For the next two years, I ascended the ranks of a company in the water treatment field, mainly selling domestic osmosis purification systems. These kinds of companies generally had their employees work independently, with income coming from sales commissions. This way, the more salespeople they had knocking on doors, the better. It meant more opportunities to get sales. Anyone was welcome; you would have had to be truly awful for the company to fire you, since it didn't cost them anything to keep you on.

Well, I met someone who was *that* awful. The guy had presented himself as a sales whiz, but he couldn't sell anything. He was claiming unemployment, though, so he hung onto the job. Finally, the company had to fire him; he was demotivating all the new salespeople. Imagine the drama.

Then - out of luck rather than strategy - this guy decided to take advantage of his last few months on unemployment to write a book. And what did he write about? Sales! Imagine! And how do I know this? Because a colleague of mine who carried on working for the company after I left called me a few years later and told me the following story:

The company had scheduled a training trip to Barcelona for all the managers. There, they would spend

> two days attending a series of conferences on sales techniques delivered by the biggest sales experts in the world.
>
> Guess who one of those speakers was?
>
> The really awful guy! And he had the balls to tell them all that he had been kicked out of his job for not making sales, and that he had gone on to write a book and now spent his days giving talks and advising salespeople for big companies.
>
> My friend told me: "Dude, after the conference I went over to talk to him and found out he earned more for that 45-minute talk than what I earn in a good sales month. And he delivers two to five conferences a month!"

Like I said, it was really crazy. This is a clear example of a snake oil salesman, which I talk about a lot in *Branding Secrets*.

I'm not using this example to encourage you to become a snake oil salesman by writing a book as a starting point. I just want to show you that not only can you write without considering yourself an expert, but **you can actually succeed with your book**. Let go of your fears and do it!

3. I'm not a writer (or I don't like to write, or I don't know how).

When I was at school, if someone had told me I would one day write a book, become an international bestselling author and end up helping people from all over the world to write their own books *and live off them*, I would have thought they were insane.

As I explained, expressive capabilities were never my strong point, as well as my spelling difficulties and my doctor's handwriting. Fortunately for me (and for you), these days, you DON'T need to be a great writer to be able to make a living from your books. **All you need is a message to spread**: knowledge or experience that can help other people.

If - like me - you don't like writing or you're not good at it, leave the technical side to your editor (we'll look at this later on). **You just focus on writing a draft of what you actually want to say**. You can also record yourself speaking if you prefer, and then have someone else transcribe it or use a free IT program to do it.

You can even go a step further. It's no secret that many writers, once they achieve fame with one of their books, start using the services of a ghostwriter. If you're not familiar with the term, a ghostwriter is simply a professional author hired to write on someone else's behalf to be published under that person's name.

Until recently, this was an elitist service that was hard to access - but today, you can find it with a simple Google search.

Not only can you find freelance ghostwriters - there are also real platforms full of professional authors ready to write your book for you for just a few cents per word. Do you really think those politicians and celebrities could write a six-hundred-word book?

Every time the thought enters your mind that you can't write a book, ***remember that Paris Hilton wrote a New York Times Bestseller***.

4. The myth of the printed book.

When you start to seriously consider writing a book, one of the first fears you have is often "a book should be at least X pages long", "I don't have that much to say", "I need to gather more material in order to write a decent book", and so on.

I was in the same boat myself. When I started writing my first book, I was convinced I didn't have that much to say and that I would only end up writing a few pages. This only got worse when I found out that Amazon - the platform I had chosen to self-publish on - required at least a hundred pages in order to be hardback. How could I publish a book that wasn't in hardback? It would be little more than a pamphlet!

Let me tell you something that will quickly help you past this stumbling block.

Firstly:

Though you may feel you don't have much to say, once you start writing, you'll see that your real problem is being able to stop: knowing what to exclude from your book so that it's not too long and boring.

If, for some reason, this doesn't happen, and your book ends up rather thin (though I really doubt it), you have several tricks at your disposal:

- Make the font a little bigger.
- Choose a font that naturally takes up more space.
- Increase your line or paragraph spacing.
- Select a smaller book format - Amazon (KPD) offers a wide range of sizes.
- Include photos, drawings and diagrams, but make sure they add value and are properly integrated.

You'll see it's easy to reach a hundred pages and get your hardback by following these simple tips - although, as I said, this probably won't be necessary. I tend to write quite concisely, so I calculated that by this point in this book, I would have written around ten pages. I haven't done my clean-up yet, but I'm at over fifty. Trust me when I say that you will be more likely to go on for too long than to struggle to write enough.

And secondly:

Not only is it hard for writers to find the time to write, it's also getting harder for readers to find the time to sit down and read. That's why short books are becoming more popular - so much so that Amazon has created a special category for them, known as "short reads". These titles take between eleven minutes and two hours to read.

Finally, let me share with you some interesting facts that will help you overcome your fear of writing a book that's "too short":

- For non-fiction books, people prefer a total of somewhere between ten thousand and twenty thousand words.
- Readers are far more likely to finish a short book than a longer one. People want books that focus on a specific issue rather than huge tomes that take on every single aspect of a topic.
- It's easier to market several shorter books than one long one.
- Having several books in an Amazon category rather than a single long book will help you to dominate that category.

5. I don't have time.

I've left this excuse till last because I hear it the most often: "I have no time", or "writing a book is too much work".

Firstly, with the right system in place, writing a book is not much work, so it doesn't matter if you're short on time.

I myself **wrote and published this and another four books in under three months** while also launching my first crowdfunding campaign, managing the manufacture of XQUAT® (the world's first portable professional gym), advising two large companies on their purchase funnel and three clients on their book launches, starting out in long-term stock market investment and finishing my *Coaching Behaviour Change* certification. Phew! And, of course, I still had time for Netflix, my weekly workout, meditating at least three times a week, reading, going out for drinks, and so on.

In this book, I'm going to show you how you can finish yours in just 30 days by dedicating around an hour a day to it, even if - like me - you're on a tight schedule.

As you can see, you don't need a Nobel Prize for Literature or all the free time in the world to write a book. All you need is to set aside an hour a day to "do your homework". In other words: **all you need to write a book is a little discipline**.

In any case, if you want to write a book but you know perseverance isn't your strong point, I would love to help you out personally, and charge dearly. I've helped so many people get in shape (as a personal trainer) or finish their books simply by being there to remind them that it's time to write or to go for a run. It's an expensive alarm, but a highly effective one. If you need that, call me! ;)

CHAPTER 3

What to write: how to find the perfect idea for your book

(Step 3)

One of the things I hear most, from friends and acquaintances as well as from clients, is: “I’d love to write a book, but I don’t know what to write it about.”

Whether this is you or, on the contrary, you have dozens of ideas and just don’t know which one to start with, you should find this chapter tremendously useful. Even if you’re clear on what book you want to write (which is a great start), doing the exercise I’m about to suggest might help you find a good focus for starting to write.

4 strategies for finding the perfect idea for your book

1. What things do people tend to ask you?

(Knowledge)

Obviously, if you're a lawyer, doctor, physiotherapist, or whatever else, people around you probably constantly bombard you with questions about your profession - but you don't need a college degree. I'm sure that my neighbor, who started going to the gym less than six months ago and has pumped his body full of more chemicals than a racehorse, gets asked much more than me - with my college education in health and sport and over twenty years of working out under my belt - how to get biceps bigger than your head or the best ab exercises.

I'm sure that you're an "expert" at something, too. Remember: just knowing a little more than someone else about a topic makes you an expert in that person's eyes.

Think about it: what do people tend to ask you about? Do you make a mean lasagne and everyone wants the recipe for it? Have you started a blog or website? Did you lose thirty pounds through a good diet and even better sex? Do you know how to get free stuff through Amazon (my cousin has a real gift for it)?

It doesn't matter how simple it seems or how easily you can find information by searching online. If you can save people's time by expressing your knowledge in a coherent, organized manner, lots of people will be prepared to pay for it.

2. Obstacles and challenges you've faced.

(Experiences)

This type of knowledge and experience is highly valued. Nothing sells better than "I hit rock bottom and still came out on top"-type stories. It's a resource often used in persuasive writing and copywriting and known as "hero's journey", and it lends authority and credibility that can turn an ordinary book into a real bestseller.

Ask yourself what difficult situations you've been in over the course of your life. Did you overcome a domestic violence situation? Did you beat alcohol or drug addiction? Have you had cancer? Maybe just reading these questions has your hair standing on end (especially if it's a subject close to home for you). Imagine the power these kinds of books can possess.

But there's no need to be dramatic about it. I wrote this book during the 2020 state of emergency during which we had to isolate in our houses for over thirty days. If you went through lockdown too, I'm sure you have a challenge to write about.

How I went through self-isolation...

- ...and used the time to write a book?
- ...without going stir crazy?
- ...and got in shape?
- ...without getting a divorce?
- Etc.

3. The things you like.

(Interests)

Want to know the easiest way to find a topic for your book? Take a look at:

- The books on your bookshelf.
- The magazines you read.
- The websites you visit.
- The shows you watch.
- Etc.

You probably already spend a lot of your time reading, watching and consuming all kinds of material related to what you like, and it would be a great topic for your own book.

Do you love running and own every copy of *Runner's World*? You could write a book compiling all the best tips and diet tricks for people who want to start running.

Do you, like my mother, watch every reality show about refurbishing, decorating, renting or selling houses? (And when I say she watches all of them, I mean ALL). You could write a book about how to decorate your house on a shoestring to increase its value.

The best part of this strategy is that you'll enjoy doing the research for your book as you'll be learning more about something you're already passionate about.

4. What things others are interested in.

(Benefits)

If there's nothing people tend to ask you about, you haven't overcome any obstacles to write home about, and you don't have an interest in any particular subject (which would surprise me), there's still no need to worry. You can write about other people's interests.

This has a big advantage when it comes to selling your book (not so much when it comes to writing it in the first place), because you're writing about a topic that you already know people are prepared to pay to read about.

So how do you know what these topics are?

1. Amazon categories and subcategories.

Go to the book department on Amazon and start navigating through the menu on the left. There, you'll find subcategories you had no idea existed. If there is a considerable number of books on a certain topic in Amazon's categories, you can bet your ass that there's an audience for it, no matter how weird you might personally find it.

2. Published magazines.

The editorial business side of magazine publishing lives off companies paying to have ads within their pages. The way to convince these companies to hire their services is to show them there is a large segment of the population interested in their subject - so, going down to the newsagent and taking a look at their magazine selection is a great way to get ideas on what to write about in order to have guaranteed potential customers.

3. **Online courses on Udemy, Skillshare, etc.**

More and more people, when deciding to learn something new, opt for online courses - especially on platforms like Udemy, which offer great courses for less than the price of a book. This means the variety and quality of these courses is getting bigger all the time, and these platforms are an amazing place to find ideas for your book.

Brainstorming

Now that you know four different strategies for finding a good idea for your book, it's time to get to it. All you need to do is set aside fifteen to thirty minutes in your diary to sit down with a pen and paper.

During this time, write as many ideas as you can for each of the four strategies we just looked at. I'm sure that some will produce more ideas than others, but try to write down at least five for each one.

It's important to use a pen and paper for this part, rather than a laptop or phone (and this is coming from a compulsive techie). The process of writing by hand engages a different part of your brain, which can help you to have even more ideas.

How to choose which book to write first

While some people may find it hard to come across a good idea they can turn into a book, others might have the opposite problem. It sounds like a great problem to have, but it can lead to what is known as "analysis paralysis".

If this sounds like you, ask yourself the following:

- Which idea would you most like to write about?

- Which book do you think will sell the most?

- Which book can you finish fastest?

I ask myself these three questions both when it comes to writing a book and when I'm creating a new project (in the latter case, I also ask myself "which requires the least investment?").

Depending on the situation you're in, some of these points are more valid than others. If, for example, you've just found yourself out of a job and you need some income to cover your basic needs, you should, of course, focus on the book that will sell the most copies.

It may be that all your needs are covered and what you're looking for is self-actualization through sharing something you're passionate about with the world. Or maybe you've taken a little time off work and your priority is to finish the book as fast as possible before you go back to work.

Given that each question carries weight, it can help to use a table:

	Book 1	Book 2	Book 3	...
What idea would you most like to write about?				
What book do you think would sell the best?				
What book could you finish most quickly?				

Assign a value from 1 to 3 to each question and each book. Once you've finished, add up the values and you'll get a book view of which book you should start with.

If you're in a place where some questions carry more weight than others, like in the examples I gave, then double your value for them - 2, 4, or 6, instead of 1, 2, or 3.

If you've done the exercise and still don't know which book to write, don't worry. Take a few days' break and come back to it. Remember that many budding writers have to do this exercise multiple times before their brainwave finally happens.

And finally... Don't get stressed.

Even if you spend a month or two writing a book that doesn't hit the *New York Times* bestseller list, you will still:

- Have an asset that can generate recurrent passive income for you.
- Have learned a lot about the book-writing process.
- Have much more confidence when it comes to starting a new book.

So, once you've done the exercise at least a couple of times, choose the book that feels right for you *now*. You can always come back and do it again later, with some more learning under your belt.

CHAPTER 4

The title: secret to success n°1

(Step 4)

You might think that writing a great book —a book people love— guarantees your success. Well, I'm sorry to say this isn't always the case - especially if you're an unknown writer.

Did you know that the first novel of Joanne Rowling, the creator of Harry Potter, was rejected by twelve publishing houses before eventually turning her into the first female writer in history to become a billionaire? Do you know how much Joanne earned from her book from the time she wrote it to when it finally fell into her readers hands, five years later? That's right...nothing!

Clearly, having a book people love and a book people buy are NOT the same thing. To earn money from your book, whether it's good or not so much, you have to reach your readers first.

Until now, whether or not your book reaches potential readers depended on a stupid publishing house deciding that your book was worthy of being published - and believe me, there are plenty of stupid publishing houses (like the twelve idiots that rejected Harry Potter). It's just like the stupid banks who laughed in the faces of Steve Jobs or Amazon's Jeff Bezos over forty times.

Luckily for you, nowadays, you don't need a publishing house to help you reach your readers and decide your book is worthy - *all you have to do is upload your book to Amazon and let them promote it for you!*

Unlike going through a traditional publishing house, this does not require any ass-kissing; no one has to like you, nor do you have to be lucky enough for that one specific person to like your book (someone who might be embittered by their own writing failures, or just plain having a bad day).

For Amazon to promote your book, all you have to do is do things right. And this starts with **your book's title.** It doesn't matter how well-written your book is or its ability to change lives and revolutionize the world - if Amazon doesn't show it to its potential readers, that's the end of the story. Period. Finito.

5 keys for winning over Amazon (and your readers) with the title of your book.

1. Keep an eye on the competition.

What better place to start than the titles of your competition? I can say from experience that most of the titles you'll see can be classified in one of the following three ways:

1. **100% SEO[7]-oriented**. You want search engines to favor you and put you in key positions, but don't forget you're writing for people, not just algorithms.

2. **Excessively creative**. Grabbing people's attention is important, but it's also important that when someone reads the title of your book, they know what the hell it's about!

3. **Boring**. Many authors decide on their books' titles while trying not to stand out too much, thinking that will help them reach as many people as possible. What they don't realize is that **if you're writing for everybody, you're not writing for anybody.**

The aim of keeping an eye on the competition is to give you an idea of the general tone of books in your field and **avoid making the same mistakes they have**. Of course, well-known writers can afford to use both hugely boring and excessively creative titles and still sell thousands of copies - but you and I have to do our homework.

---

[7] SEO stands for search engine optimization, which is a set of practices designed to improve the appearance and positioning of web pages in organic search results.

2. Minimum viable SEO.

There is no faster or more effective way to ensure your book will be shown to your potential clients than by using keywords - or SEO techniques - in its title. Why is it so important to use keywords?

- Keywords determine your book's positioning on Amazon.

- Keywords determine your book's ranking on Google.

- Keywords determine how many Amazon pages your book will appear on - for example, "customers also bought...".

Of all the keywords in your book, the most important ones are in the title. Don't worry - to have a good SEO strategy, all you need to do is follow these simple steps:

- Google the phrase "Google Keyword Planner" and select the first result that appears.

- Click "Go to Keyword Planner".

- If you don't have an account, you'll need to create one by going to "New Google Ads Account" (don't worry, it's free).

- Click "Discover new keywords", write down all the words and phrases that come to mind related to your topic, and click "Get results".

- Click on “Average monthly searches”. This will organize your results by search volume.

- Choose between ten and fifteen results that have at least a thousand searches a month and that could be used as a basis for your book title. Choose ones with low competition or, at the very least, medium.

Now that you have your list of keywords, you can move on to the next part.

3. Hit the sore points.

We open our wallets unthinkingly in order to relieve a current sore point (those extra pounds, a relationship break-up, and so on). But we think about it much more when it’s about relieving a future sore point. They sell more aspirin than vitamins, put it that way.

Your title should focus on the main sore points your book can resolve for your readers: what can it do for them, and why should they be interested? First, find out your target audience’s main sore point, and then create a title that tells them you can relieve it.

4. Show your personality.

If you've read my book Branding Secrets, you'll know I place a lot of stock in the idea of "brand differentiation". This term is rooted in the notion that it's more important (and lucrative) to be **different** than to be **better**.

Don't be afraid to show your personality: it's a hugely potent weapon that will enable you to differentiate yourself and stand out from the competition. Let me give you an example:

a) 100% SEO title: How to write a book: writing and publishing a book on Amazon.

b) SEO + Personality: How to write and publish a book on Amazon for people who hate writing.

You might think the latter title is risky. Many people believe that if you hate writing, you're not a real writer or that you should find other work. You might be thinking this title could cost you a lot of potential customers. But I'll say it again (I had to hear it several times before I finally got it):

If you're writing for everybody, you're not writing for anybody.

5. Include a time frame.

Now you have a title with all the elements necessary to win Amazon around, thanks to the minimum viable SEO you've applied, hitting your readers' sore points, and standing out from the competition with a splash of personality.

Your potential client is now clear on what they can expect from your book - all that's left is to tell them when they will get that result. We live in a here-and-now society, so it's inevitable that your prospective customer will wonder when they can expect to see the promised benefits. Why not answer their question before they've even asked it?

There are myriad expressions you can use: "in less than an hour", "in 30 days"... Just be careful not to create unrealistic expectations.

Now that we've gone through everything, you can put it all together and apply the following, **Formula for the Perfect Title**:

FPT = keywords (SEO) + solution (sore point) + personality + time frame.

Bear in mind that you won't always be able to or want to use each and every one of these elements. That's why I advise you to create at least two combinations and do a little poll among your friends and family to help you take a step back and have the best chances of success.

At this point, you have a good driving force to help you overcome any writers' block that might crop up along the way, you've hit upon the perfect idea for your (first) book, and you've created a super-title that inspires you and keeps you focused. **It's time to write.**

CHAPTER 5

How to write your book

(Step 5)

As I confessed earlier, I've always considered writing to be among my biggest weak points. The fact that it took my first book - at just over thirty thousand words long - four years to finish is proof of that. I could never have imagined that one day I would be writing books for a living - much less that I would be helping others to do the same.

Luckily, the day I decided I wanted to turn writing into a way of life (rather than a four-year torment for each book), I had a very powerful weapon, and one I consider to be my greatest superpower: LAZINESS.

I'm a very **persistent** person (or stubborn, whatever) and if I set out to do something, I find a way to do it. But I'm also **tremendously lazy**. The mix of these two opposing qualities has a wonderful result: I always find the easiest way to get what I want.

This efficient way of doing things is actually known as the **Pareto Principle** or **80/20 Rule**. It means that generally speaking, and for a wide range of phenomena, approximately **80% of consequences come from 20% of causes**.

- 80% of wealth is accumulated by 20% of the population.

- 80% of a hospital's resources are used by 20% of its patients.

- 80% of a company's revenue comes from 20% of its clients.

- 20% of the carpet in your house or office gets 80% of the foot traffic.

- Etc.

Applying this principle to the academic field enabled me to always be top of the class despite being one of the students who spent the least time studying, and in sports it allowed me to be one of the most "ripped" at the gym even though I worked out a fraction as much as the others.

What I mean by this is that spending less time on a task but doing it in the most efficient way won't give you worse results - quite the opposite. Focusing on the most important aspects of the task rather than trying to take on the whole thing will get you

better results with less effort. We're going to apply this when it comes to writing your book.

To do this, I've developed a **simple 3-step** system: create a **mind map**, do a little **research** and draw up a **blueprint**.

1. The magic of mind maps.

For this first part, we're going to employ a tool widely used to extract information: mind maps.

When you complete this exercise, you'll realize that you have much more to write about than you could have possibly imagined. If you take it seriously and dedicate enough time to it, your book will virtually write itself.

Just like we did with your book's title, when it comes to creating a mind map, it helps to use a pen and paper to stimulate your creativity and give you more ideas than doing it digitally.

The first thing you have to do is write your title (the main idea) in the middle of your sheet of paper and then draw a circle around it. Now, it's time to juice your memory and creativity: start by making notes around the title of all the ideas that pop into your head relating to your book's topic, connecting to that inner circle by lines. Think about the different areas your book could discuss: examples, personal experiences, articles you've read or saved, movies...

As you note down these main ideas or themes, you'll think of new sub-themes related to them. Draw a new circle around the main ideas and note these subtopics around them just like you did with the book title, and so on and so forth. You can use colors, drawings, cuttings, and more.

Your mind map should start to look like this:

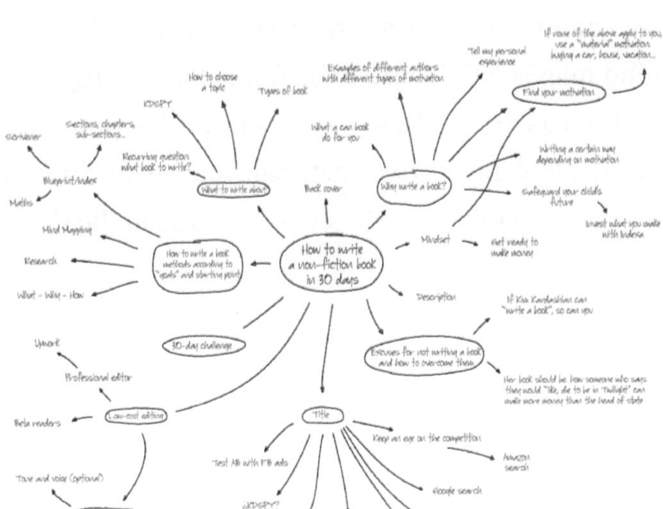

Keep drawing circles and lines to new ideas for as long as you can: fifteen minutes minimum. Set a timer if you have to.

If you run out of paper, don't hesitate to grab another sheet and keep expanding your mind map as much as you can. I've seen mind maps bigger than a king-size bed, so don't hold back.

There are two rules to bear in mind while you're completing this exercise:

1. **No filters.**

Don't limit your imagination; any idea that comes to mind is a valid one. Nothing is extraneous, nothing too crazy.

2. Leave perfectionism at the door.

If your mind map isn't a total mess...you're doing it wrong! Your mind map is NOT there to be framed and hung on a wall - it's for getting as many ideas out of your head as you can. If you try to make it look pretty or structured, you will be limiting your creativity. There will be time to shape it a little in the third step.

2. The power of research.

Now that you've squeezed the right side of your brain, it's time to put the more analytical left side to use. Now is the time to activate your investigative superpowers.

When it comes to the ESSENTIAL task of research, I've come across two types of writer:

a) **Those who love research** (or are mega-perfectionists, like me). They can spend months or even years (I'm proof) looking for every snippet of information on the subject they want to write about. Their books may never see the light of day.

b) **Those who skip research.** These authors find the research process so unbelievably tedious that they just go with their instincts and skip it altogether.

Striking a balance between too much and too little research is one of the challenges you'll face on the exciting journey to writing your book.

To finish your mind map with some important ideas or points you might have forgotten or not known about, and to **avoid falling into analysis paralysis during the research stage**, we're going to use Pareto's Principle, or 80/20 Rule that we looked at at the beginning of this chapter. The hardest part of applying this principle is working out which are the 20% of tasks with the potential to get 80% of the results.

I present to you: "the Holy Trinity of research for non-fiction writers".

- Kindle's content index.
- Amazon reviews.
- The top three books in your field (optional).

a) Kindle's content index.

Go on Amazon, look for the ten highest-selling books in your book's category or field, and click "Look inside".

Once you're in, all you have to do is go to the index or contents page. Within the *Holy Trinity* of research for non-fiction writers, this is, without a doubt, the Holy Grail.

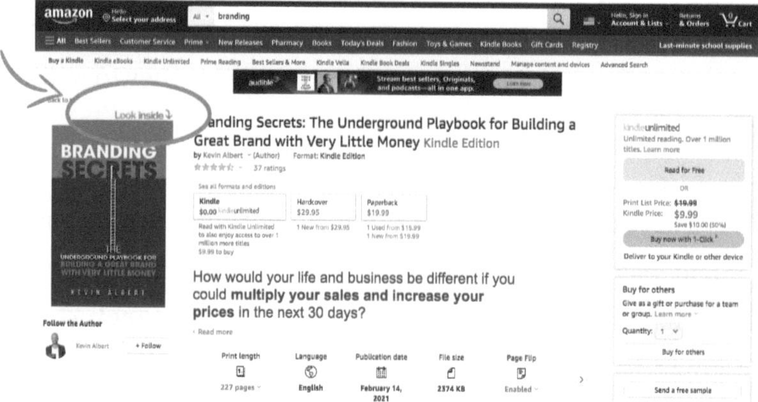

Where to find the "Look inside" butto

As well as noting down on your mind map any new ideas you come across while looking through the contents of these ten bestsellers, this point will also enable you to see:

- The number of sections, chapters and subchapters that tend to be necessary for your book's topic.

- Which chapters/ideas are included across all the books.

- Which chapters/ideas are NOT included in all of them. Maybe your book doesn't need them either (we'll find that out in the next point: Amazon reviews).

- How many pages (or words) tend to be devoted to each aspect.

Note: Just because you're noting down new ideas from these contents tables in your mind map, doesn't mean you have to write about them in your book. You can decide that later, and it will depend on your strategy.

b) Amazon reviews.

This method of research will enable you to go from a "complete" book to a book people actually love. What's more, unlike the contents page method, almost nobody does this.

If you do your homework right, discarding boring or generic reviews ("I love this book", "I hate this book", "This book didn't arrive on time", and the like) and focus on the specific, detailed reviews, you can figure out:

- **What points your readers felt were lacking**. If you find several readers complaining that a certain type of information was missing from all or most of the books on your chosen topic, you've stumbled upon a gold mine: take advantage of it to differentiate yourself and stand out from the competition.

- **What points you can skip**. Maybe you can skip over excessively basic aspects or omit any that are overly technical. Always keep in mind the audience you're writing for. Don't try to tackle everything. Less is more.

- **What aspects readers truly grasped**. Maybe it's the books' clarity or structure, maybe it's the use of examples, maybe it's that they felt they could relate to the writer. Pay attention and take note.

- **What aspects readers were annoyed by**. It may be something as simple as correcting grammar mistakes or not generating unrealistic expectations with the books' titles. Try to avoid those pitfalls.

c) **The three best books in your field** (optional).

If you're thinking about writing a book, you've probably already read the top titles in your chosen field - if you haven't, I strongly recommend that you do. You probably won't find any ideas beyond what you found in their indexes or reviews (although you might), but you need to know who you're up against. It's not that you're going to copy them or try to go one better, but you do need to get an idea of **what made these books nº 1** and, above all, **how you can stand out**.

If your mind map was already kind of tangled before you even began your research process, it will probably be total chaos by the time you finish it. Don't worry; that's pretty normal. It's time to give method to the madness.

Pro tip: this is somewhat optional, but once I've "finished" writing up my mind map, I spend half an hour typing it up on an online app like *MindNode*[8] (available for cellphone and PC). This means that when I get a new idea, I can easily add it to the map. Carrying a king-size version around with you isn't awfully practical.

IMPORTANT! Not taking enough of an interest in creating this mind map can lead you to spend hours upon hours sitting in front of a blank page, banging your head against the wall trying to think of what the hell you're going to write.

Failing to create a mind map will probably lead to failing to create your book. Don't make that mistake.

---

[8] soykevinalbert.com/mindmap

3. Blueprint structure.

Once you've sampled the magic of mind maps and added your *minimum viable research*, it's time to give the magic some structure. We're going to turn your chaotic mind map into a structured, easy-to-follow blueprint that will serve as your GPS.

Just like how your GPS will stop you from having to slam the brakes on your car every time you reach an intersection or have to lean out the window to ask someone which road leads to Rome (I promise that when it comes to writing a book, not all of them will), the blueprint for your book will help you to relax along the way and enjoy the writing journey.

To turn your mind map into a good GPS (not one of those that yell "turn!" when you're halfway down the highway), we're going to put it through three simple checks.

Check 1: Find the sections, chapters and subchapters.

The first thing you need to do is take a step back and gain some perspective. Don't let yourself not see the wood for the trees. Are you able to distinguish the main topics or sections into which you'll divide your book?

Grab a fresh sheet of paper and write these sections at the top, as headings. Once you've done this, I want you to put the rest of your ideas (all of them) under the section they fit best with. If you find that an idea fits into more than one section, add it to both and connect them with arrows.

Once you've written all your ideas in, draw a circle around those that can be used as chapters in your book, and join them with lines to the subchapters or main points to talk about for each.

Your blueprint will start to look like this:

WRITE YOUR BOOK	PUBLISH YOUR BOOK	SELL YOUR BOOK
How to write your book	Self-publishing vs publishing house	How to get reviews
Title	Why choose Amazon	Amazon bestseller in 24h
What to write	Cover	AMS: Amazon marketing
Description	KDSPY	Divide and conquer
Why write a book	Back cover	Play with prices
The magic of blueprints	Description	Lead-magnet
The power of research	How to set a price	Affiliations
How to write a book		

Don't be afraid to leave ideas out; we're in the middle of the distillation process, and this is what's supposed to happen. If your book can do without elements that are either very basic or very advanced, don't hesitate to cross them off. You don't have to create the most advanced book on a given topic; you just have to create a book that's different from others on your chosen subject.

Remember: Different is better than better.

Note: if your book is not very long, you may not need to create sections; the headings for this initial blueprint can be the chapters themselves.

Check 2: Digitalize your blueprint in a logical sequence.

Once you've identified your sections, chapters and subchapters, it's time to move from paper to computer. All you have to do while digitalizing your blueprint is order all of these points in a logical sequence that will allow readers to easily follow your book's flow. Start with the sections, then complete them by adding chapters and, finally, subchapters.

You may need to go beyond these subchapters and incorporate points and sub-points. Go into as much depth as necessary. These points and sub-points don't need to be included in your book's contents page, but they will help you when it comes to writing.

Check 3: Do the math.

It's time for our final check, which will result in your "definitive" blueprint/index which you will use to begin working on your book. For this last check, you're going to need a calculator.

Have you already thought about how many pages you want your book to have? If not, now is the time to do it. You can use your favorite books as a benchmark or refer to the bestsellers in your field (the ones you researched in the previous stage). Now, I'm going to explain why.

Let's say you want to write a thirty-thousand-word book. Now, divide this number into the number of chapters in your blueprint. This calculation will tell you how many words each chapter needs to contain.

Why do these numbers matter?

- Once you know how many words you can write per hour, you'll know how long you should dedicate each day to your book in order to finish in the time you've set yourself.

- You can reorganize all your chapters - joining some together and splitting others - if you see that there's a big imbalance between them.

- A very low number of words per chapter may indicate that it could be a good idea to divide your book into multiple books. This is a good time to do it: creating two or more blueprints based on your original blueprint. Sometimes, each section can make a great book all on its own.

If you've followed all the directions in this chapter, by now you should have an invaluable blueprint in your hands and be ready to begin your 'writer in 30 days' challenge.

If you decided to give this chapter - or the whole book - a re-read first, before starting to write (which I think is a great idea), I really want to hammer home the importance of not skipping this point. If you don't take the time to complete the steps we've looked at so far, writing your book could be a real nightmare. Preparing a good blueprint for your book might take a few hours or even days. but it will save you months or years of work down the line. Please, don't try to take a shortcut here: your blueprint *is* the shortcut. I promise you'll thank me later.

CHAPTER 6

Challenge: Writer in 30 days

(Step 6)

Once you've finished your blueprint, it's time to start writing your book. In this chapter, I'm going to show you how to finish your book's first draft in 30 days or less.

To sign up for this challenge, all you have to do is commit to following two simple steps:

1. You can't start editing until you reach the end of your book.
2. You can't take on any other projects during these 30 days.

Do you accept the challenge?

Fuckeable Tournament: The birth of the "writer in 30 days" challenge.

As I've mentioned several times in this book, one of my many facets is as a personal trainer. But not just some guy who says he's a personal trainer: a real one, with certifications and everything!

With over twenty years' experience, having worked with hundreds of clients (both pro and amateur), and, above all, having applied the 80/20 Rule to my working methodology, I was able to start guaranteeing results many years ago.

Before I start work with a client, we set some objectives - usually yearly ones - and if we don't reach them, I give the customer his or her money back (ALL of it). To date, I've never had to refund any of my clients. Obviously, this is because I have a great work system... but it's also because I keep an ace up my sleeve: **challenges and contests**.

No matter how well you do things, in the world of fitness you can (and will) experience plateaus or blocks where you stop progressing for a few weeks or even months. This is pretty normal, and it's often resolved by just being patient. But, since I guarantee results and losing a year's pay leaves kind of a bitter taste, when a client reaches this point I organize a mini contest or tournament lasting a month or two.

During these tournaments, workouts don't get longer or more intense, nor do diets get stricter. But they **always** help people overcome plateaus and blockages, and sometimes even allow for more progress than the entire year prior. How is this possible?

1. **Short-term aims**. Long-term goals are, without a doubt, the most important kind - but distance in time can mean these aims lose their ability to motivate. A short-term aim is easier to measure and visualize, which amplifies its power.

2. **Intrinsic motivation**. A competitive setting involves an element of challenge that gives participants the chance to compare their skills with those of other competitors and assess their own achievements. This is why I always find another client who wants to take part, or - "worst" case scenario - they compete against me as their coach.

3. **Extrinsic motivation**. The winner, in addition to the reward inherent to having improved their appearance in record time, wins a prize agreed upon by participants in advance. Sometimes, we even throw in punishments, too :)

4. **Peer "pressure" or support**. One thing I ask of my clients during these competitions is that they post their goal on social media. When you share your objectives with people around you, it makes them more real. Feeling that people are watching your progress makes you more committed, and - of course - they'll often cheer you on, too.

So much progress can be made with these kinds of challenges that, a few years ago, I started to use them myself, and created the *Fuckeable Tournaments:* contests developed to compete against my friends and give us an extra push toward that summer body.

As I'm sure you can understand, I can't show you the tournaments of my private customers...but you can see the ones with my friends. I made it a condition of taking part that they let me share their photos ;)

Don't be scared → *www.fuckeable.com*

Seeing the potential of these challenges, I decided to design the "Writer in 30 days" challenge. It applies the same principles and very similar methodology to the fitness tournaments, and it gets the same extraordinary results in record time. As it happens, I'm writing this book right now using the very same system, and competing against my girlfriend and a friend of ours.

Impatient to find out exactly what this challenge consists of?

Writer in 30 days: The challenge.

Just like with my fitness challenges, the *Writer in 30 days* challenge helps turn a generally hard process into a stimulating journey that can even be fun.

To help you understand and follow it more easily, I've divided the challenge into 3 fundamental parts: planning, organization, and competition.

1. Planning.

a) Set a final objective.

You need to start with the end in mind. The first step will be to determine your final goal for this challenge: **to finish the first draft of your book within 30 days**.

Since you have already done your research by now and know, among other things, how many chapters your book will have and roughly how many words you want to write in total, you can now go into more depth.

Your final aim could be: **to write X number of chapters** (the total number set out in your blueprint) in 30 days or **to write X number of words** (the total number in your book) in 30 days.

b) Set a daily objective.

Let's say you want to write a 30,000-word book with 10 chapters within 30 days. The next step will be to divide this final objective into daily ones - so, divide it by 30. This means your daily goal will be to write a chapter every 3 days, or 1000 words a day.

Knowing how much you need to write each day will give you accurate insight into your progress and tell you whether or not you can achieve your goal within the specified timeframe.

c) Set weekly goals.

You may not feel like spending the same amount of time writing your book every day; some days you'll be more motivated and write much more than your daily goal, and some you'll barely be able to churn out a few words. This is why it's important to set intermediate goals or milestones.

For this challenge, it's best to divide the final goal into four and review them each week. Following the previous example, your weekly aim would be to write two and a half chapters, or 7,500 words.

2. Organization.

a) Draw up a writing timetable.

The best way to progress with your book is to plan your day in advance and schedule specific blocks of time during which you can totally focus on writing - if possible, always in the same place and at the same time. Remember, we're trying to create a routine that makes things easier for you. If you wait for free time to just pop up during the day so that you can write, you'll NEVER finish your book.

I recommend setting aside at least an hour a day. If you have more time some days and you feel inspired, keep going for as long as your schedule allows, or until your inspiration runs dry. Of course, this will depend a lot on the length of your book and on how many words you can write in an hour. When you get to the end of the first week, review your weekly goal for week 1, and adjust as needed.

Not sure how you're going to find the time? Well, I have a lot of ideas: try getting up a half hour earlier, going to bed an hour later, cutting down on TV time, social media or other leisure, skip the gym or evening classes for a month, and so on. Obviously, this will all depend on how motivated you are and how important writing your book is to you, but it's essential that you schedule your time blocks in advance.

If possible, try to write when you're most productive: the times at which you feel freshest and most creative. For some people, this is first thing in the morning after their coffee; others feel more inspired right before bed; others when they wake up from an afternoon nap, and so on. Decide what the best time is for you and try to stick to it every day.

Do the same with the place you write in. Do you focus better at home? Prefer to go to the library? Could you maybe write at the beach or a peaceful park?

Personally, I write at around ten o'clock in the morning - it takes me a while to fully wake up - at some charming little cafe or other, accompanied by my laptop and notebook. Whenever I try to do it at a different time or in a different place, my productivity suffers a lot.

b) Switch off.

In the digital age we're living in, we are always connected. Many people (including myself) feel a compulsive need to check their social media or emails on their phones. I get annoyed just seeing the badge on an app to tell me I have unread messages (it's an OCD thing for me).

These distractions can seriously damage your productivity and present a great obstacle in your writing routine. This is why it's hugely important that you switch off from everything when you sit down to write, especially if you're easily distracted.

Turn off your phone and disconnect your laptop from the wifi: two essential steps when it comes to beginning your routine. Do what it takes to ensure that the only thing you can focus on during this time is your book, and nothing else.

c) Your author routine.

Now that you know how much you need to write each day and you've scheduled your time blocks, let's look at exactly what your daily routine as an author will consist of.

Remember why you're doing this (1 min). It's as simple as it sounds. Before you start writing, remember why you decided to write this book, and jot it down. This simple exercise will help to refocus you and get you through the difficult days.

Mind map for each chapter (15 min). Every time you start a new chapter, you're going to create a miniature mind map for that specific chapter.

Grab a blank sheet of paper, write the chapter's title in the center, and draw a circle around it. Now, just like you did with your overall blueprint, draw lines coming off of this and note down any ideas you have relating to that chapter: points, sub-points, examples, stories, and so on.

Fill out your blueprint (5 min). Once you've finished this mini mind map, go back to your overall blueprint and add any new ideas you just had for that chapter.

WRITE (40-90 min). Using your blueprint as a GPS, start your timer and write for as long as you said you would. Since you already know what you're going to talk about and the sequence you'll do it in, the writing process shouldn't hold any surprises. So get scribbling!

In short, your daily routine should look like this:

1. **Why**: 1 minute.
2. **Mind map**: 15 minutes (only on days when you start a new chapter).
3. **Blueprint**: 5 minutes (as above).
4. **Write**: 40-90 minutes.

3. Competition.

a) Find your competitors.

Competing against yourself is fine. Setting daily and weekly goals to fulfil will help you get through and finish your book in the allotted time. But you can't deny that **it's fun to compete against other people, as well as highly motivational**.

One of the most important factors for a writer - especially a first-time one - to be successful (ie to finish their book) is third party supervision. I'm sure you've seen movies where the star, a successful author, experiences writers' block and would be tempted to take a year's sabbatical if not for their editor on their back day and night. Of course, he ends up meeting his deadline, his publisher renews his contract, he gets the girl and lives happily ever after.

Well, that is exactly what your competitor or competitors are going to do with you, only less annoyingly. All you need to do is schedule a couple of sessions (face-to-face or over videocall) where you can share your aims and daily or weekly progress. This will activate your competitive streak, and you'll be spurred on to keep getting better. "*If they can do it, what's stopping me?*"

In these sessions, not only do you share your goals and progress (not the same thing) with each other, but also your best practice, any difficulties you encounter along the way, tricks you've picked up, and anything you think could contribute to your own success and that of your rivals.

With the *Fuckeable* Tournaments, we don't even need to schedule these mini-sessions. Our progress - measured in weight and body fat - is recorded automatically in the cloud, since we all own the same smart scale. We all have access to each other's data. As well as this, we monitor calories in and distance walked (through the same app), which helps give us an idea of why progress is or isn't happening, and either copy other participants or help them out.

Note: If you don't know anyone in the same position as you who you could compete against, try to find someone you trust who can check on your progress every day or week.

b) Broadcast your goal to the world.

As well as sharing your goals and progress with your fellow competitors, I recommend that you share them publicly on your social media and with family and friends.

This will add some **extra commitment**. Deciding to do something, keeping it to yourself, and then changing your mind is no big deal - but it's another thing entirely to know you're going to have to explain to dozens of people that you threw in the towel on that objective you claimed was so important to you.

This will also garner you **additional support** - sometimes, from unexpected people. Maybe one of your colleagues has written a book too, and would love to follow your progress and help you along the way.

Finally, shouting it from the rooftops is an amazing (and sneaky) way to promote your book. People who get involved and follow your progress will feel like part of the project, and they'll want to buy your book when it comes out.

c) Celebrate your wins.

Getting into the habit of celebrating your achievements and wins - no matter how small - can be very powerful when it comes to accomplishing your present and future objectives.

If you've found an opponent or group of opponents to compete against, then during the first mini-session you schedule together, agree upon a prize for the winner or winner.

If you took a look at the *Fuckeable Tournaments*, you will have seen that we have an individual prize (affordable) as well as collective prizes, like a "cheat meal" together or photoshoot to immortalize our beach bodies.

If you haven't managed to find anyone to compete against, before you write a single word, decide how you're going to celebrate on day 30, when you've finished your book. Writing a book is something millions of people dream about, but only a select group of fighters ever make it. Don't undervalue what you've achieved; reward yourself like you deserve.

Once you've celebrated having finished your first draft, **it's time to edit your book.**

CHAPTER 7

Low-cost editing

(Step 7)

I know: you've just undertaken the mammoth task of writing your book (something 99% of people want to do but never will), and in record time! I know the last thing you want to do is start checking it over and correcting it, so I have good news for you: the first step in the editing process is REST. **And it's not optional**.

Celebrate having finished your book, and let a week go by. Then, it's time to dust off that draft and start sculpting it into a true work of art.

Spoiler alert: the first time you re-read your draft, it's going to seem nothing like a work of art.

During the editing process, your book will pass through three sets of hands: yours, your beta readers', and a professional editor's.

Phase 1: self-editing.

The first check needs to be done by you, and it's going to be a triple check. This means that rather than reading your book through once and trying to correct it all in one go, you're going to read it three times, paying attention to a specific aspect each time. If you try to fix it all in one go, you'll find it an uphill struggle and you'll feel like you've stalled (which you may well have done).

1. On your **first check**, all you're allowed to do is **underline and take notes** of the errors and inconsistencies you come across, in addition to any improvements you'd like to make.

2. On the **second**, you should pay attention to the **coherence and fluidity** of your text: reorganize sections or even add and take away from them as needed.

3. On your **third and final check**, all that's left is to go through your **spelling and grammar** mistakes.

That's it: your book is ready to move onto the next phase. Don't keep checking it over forever. This is one of the biggest mistakes an author can make. It's better to have a finished imperfect book than one "perfect" chapter in an unfinished book.

Don't forget: "Finished is better than perfect".

Phase 2: beta readers.

If two heads are better than one, imagine what twenty can see. Beta readers are an amazing way to get feedback during your book's editing process: finding inconsistencies and grammatical errors, giving you an idea of how your book will be received by future readers, and more.

A beta reader is basically anyone who reads your book's draft and offers you constructive feedback (beyond just "I liked it" or "I didn't like it"). Your will benefit from their corrections and suggestions, and they will get a free copy of your draft.

Your close friends and family members aren't the best beta readers, since it's hard for them to be objective; they will be trying not to hurt your feelings. That's not what you need right now.

So where can you find your beta readers? Firstly, ask around the people who have been following your book's progress during the Writer in 30 days challenge and who are interested or knowledgeable about the topic of your book.

If none or very few of your "followers" meet these requirements, you can find beta readers in Facebook groups around your topic or general non-fiction reading.

Once you've selected your beta readers, make sure that along with a digital copy of your draft, you send them some basic indications of what you're expecting from them. It could be simply underlining any grammatical errors they encounter while reading, or a short list of specific questions on the content of your book.

What should you look for in the feedback you receive? You don't have to go with every single suggestion from your beta readers when modifying your book. You can't please everyone, and trying is a big mistake. **What you're looking for are common points**. Find the suggestions that come up over and over and decide if you need to make some last-minute modifications before moving onto the third phase.

Phase 3: your professional editor.

We're almost there. We've made it to the third and final phase of editing your book and we're about to turn that chaotic draft you started checking just a few days ago into a real masterpiece.

Your book has now been through three self-checks by you and one by your beta readers, so you might be tempted to skip this last step and save a few bucks. Don't make that mistake.

Your checks and those of your beta readers have certain limitations. Having a professional editor go into depth on your work is **a very important step before you click "publish".**

A good editor can help you polish your draft, fix any small (or not so small) faux pas, and offer you suggestions on how to improve your book. It's easy to find a professional editor, but getting it cheap is less easy. Fortunately, I wrote a whole book on precisely this.

Of all the places where you can find an editor for your book, I recommend *Upwork*[9], a virtual marketplace that puts the best freelancers from all over the world in touch with companies or individuals looking for talented professionals.

Basically, all you have to do is sign up to the platform and post your job offer (editing your book) following the steps the site tells you to. You'll start getting proposals from dozens of freelancers interested in editing your book. Your only task is to find the professional offering the best quality for the best price.

How to choose your editor

The best thing about working with a platform like Upwork is that you can check the profiles of all the freelancers offering to edit your book: their rates, training, portfolios, and, above all, their reviews.

You could get lost in all the information on show and spend days reading profiles. But you don't need to. Here's how I do it:

First, I discard proposals from any freelancers who have earned less than $12,000 on the platform or who have a client satisfaction rating of under 90%. Already, this will reduce your

---

[9] *upwork.com*

shortlist to just a few offers. Among the professionals still standing, take a look to see if any of them specialize in, or have background in, your book's topic. Mark them as your favorites.

All that's left to do now is discuss prices.

How much does it cost to edit a book with Upwork?

The answer is simple: however much you want to spend.

For years now, I've used Upwork for one thing or another almost every week (you can't imagine the scope of the things you can commission there). The first thing I learned about working with these platforms is that, just like in the offline world, prices vary *to infinity and beyond.*

For the same book (thirty thousand words, let's say), two freelancers with the same degree of training and experience might charge you a hundred dollars or over five thousand.

Official prices for editing a book are generally considered to be between $0.005 and $0.015 per word, as recommended by the Editorial Freelancers Association. But that doesn't mean you won't find rates far higher or lower with similar results. This abysmal difference depends on various factors, the main one being the freelancer's country of origin, since it's more expensive to live in the US than in, say, Thailand. But it can also depend on how in-demand or "famous" the freelancer is.

But don't be disheartened; this is the beauty of these marketplaces. Remember: if a professional has 90% client satisfaction or higher and has earned at least $12,000 on the platform, it's almost guaranteed that they will do a good job.

To help give you an idea, for my last few books (of between fifteen and thirty thousand words each), I paid on average $95.

And there you have it!

If your book has been through the three phases of editing (self-editing, beta readers and professional editing), you've finished your book.

CONGRATULATIONS! You did it!

If you're a super-perfectionist like me and you're tempted to keep checking your book over and over again, unnecessarily delaying its launch (just in case you find something you can improve on or some grammatical mistake to correct), remember: Amazon lets you keep making modifications to your book FOREVER, even after it's been published!

So, there's no excuse. If you followed all the steps in this first section, I'm sure you have a masterpiece on your hands, and it deserves to see the light of day. Don't deprive the world of this privilege, and don't deprive yourself of the satisfaction.

It's time to publish your book.

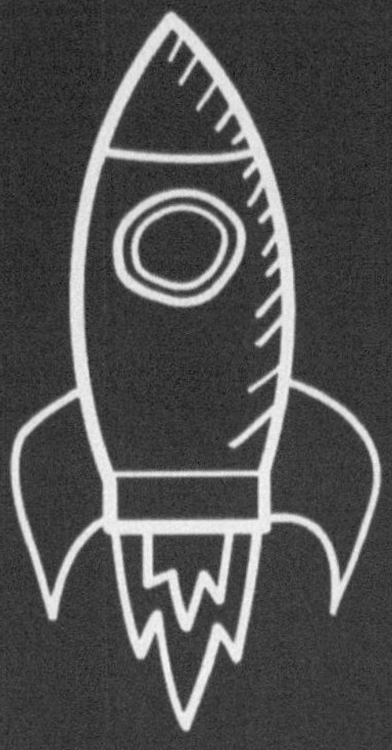

PUBLISH YOUR BOOK

- A 7-STEP GUIDE TO SELF-PUBLISHING ON AMAZON -

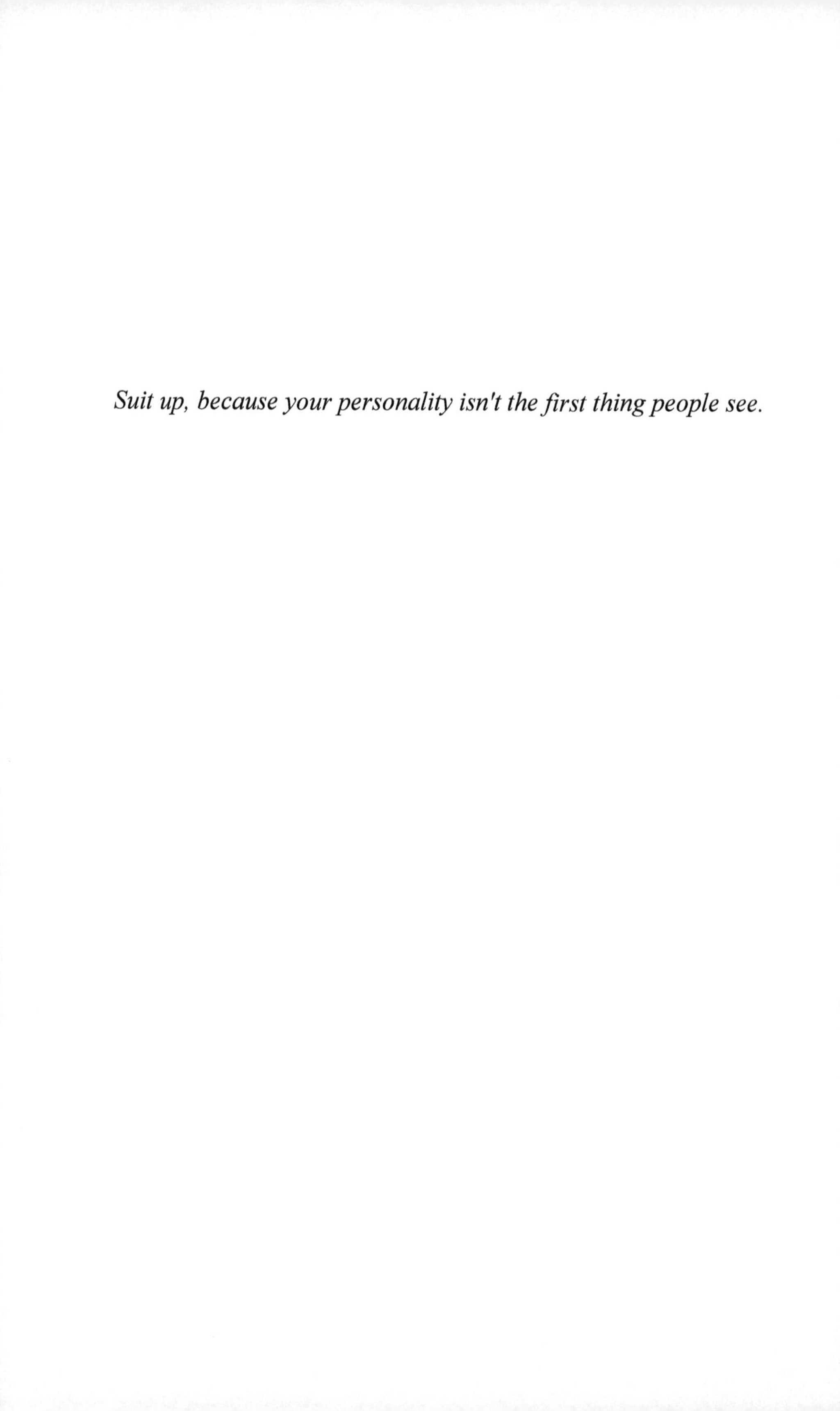

Suit up, because your personality isn't the first thing people see.

Introduction

Having spent four long years writing my first book, in early 2016 I finally finished the last of dozens of corrections that my obsessive-compulsive disorder had forced me to subject my work to before considering it ready to see the light of day. My moment had finally come. Before I knew it, my book would be published.

At least, that's what I thought. But it wasn't until the middle of that year, some six months later, that the book finally went on sale. Is it really necessary for so much time to pass between finishing a book and seeing it published?

Well, THAT DEPENDS.

Let's look at two extreme scenarios: if you throw yourself at the mercy of a publishing house, your masterpiece may end up being published years after your death (it happened to J.R.R. Tolkien with *The Lord of the Rings*), but if you self-publish without taking care over the details, you can do it in under thirty minutes.

Neither of these two routes are very promising: the former because you will never enjoy the success your book may achieve, and the latter because your rush to get published without crossing the t's and dotting the i's is normally a guarantee you'll fail.

Is there a middle ground? Is it possible to publish a book without waiting months or years for a company to consider you worthy of publishing but to do it with the same guarantee of success?

Yes, THERE IS.

And that, my friend, is the aim of this section: I am going to show you how I went from publishing my first book in just over six months, to doing it in under a week and with **maximum chances of success**.

CHAPTER 8

Self-publishing vs Publishing houses

As you know, I ended up self-publishing my first book *Branding Secrets* on Amazon. Making this decision was what delayed the launch of my book by six long months, not the typical delays of a publishing company.

I'm someone who, when making an important decision, analyzes every possible variable. Of course, having dedicated over four years to writing my book, this was undoubtedly a fundamental decision, and not one I was prepared to leave to chance. So, as usual, I did my homework.

Although I tend to begin my research online, I had become a real expert during my work on my first book, so I had close links with many other experts (in and out of the world of branding) who just "happened" to have one or more published books.

So, the first step in my investigation consisted of meeting with six of these experienced authors in order to ask them what route they had chosen to take (publishing house or doing it themselves) and how they had found it.

I don't know what surprised me more: discovering that they had all published their books through a company, or finding out their reasons for doing it. Five of them agreed that going through a publishing house "gives you more cachet".

If I wasn't disconcerted enough at these initial findings, the next discovery left me shellshocked: five of the six (yes, the same ones who said "cachet") **had paid to have their books published**. And not small change: some of them admitted to me that **publishing had involved a financial investment they would probably never recoup through book sales**.

WHAT THE HELL?! To get published, I had to get into debt?! That's not what happens in the movies!

I thought that if you wrote a good book and were "lucky" enough for a publishing house to like it and get behind it, they would take care of absolutely everything: give you a check and a percentage of the sales, and all you had to do was sign books in Barnes & Noble.

Either I was an idiot... or something strange was happening here.

And it turned out, something strange was happening.

Luckily for my research, one of these six experts had not had to pay to publish their work and could confirm to me that in fact, things worked very similarly to what I had thought (without the Barnes & Noble part). They explained to me, although their initial paycheck was for less than $2000 and their annual royalties close to zero, **a publishing house never asks you for money to publish your book.**

The other people I talked to had fallen for what's known as the "publishing scam". Roughly speaking, it consists of a **printing house**, which makes money by printing stuff, presenting themselves as a **publishing house**, which makes money by selling books. It doesn't matter if they call it **co-publishing** or **self-publishing** – if you have to pay *anything* to publish your book, IT'S A PRINTING HOUSE.

If you want to find out more about the topic, just google "publishing scam" and you can read all about these con artists. You'll find personal stories of rage and frustration that I hope will help stop you from falling into their **perfectly designed trap**.

Having got to this point, and with the information I had obtained, I had two options:

1. I could publish my book through a printing house in less than a month, spending a few thousand dollars[10].

---

[10] The authors I spoke to spent between $5000 and $20,000.

2. I could spend months contacting "real" publishing houses and crossing my fingers that one would do me the "favor" of publishing my book and paying me two thousand measly dollars plus some practically non-existent royalties[11].

Looking at this unencouraging panorama, all I could do was use my entrepreneurial spirit and discover the self-publishing route for myself.

As you can probably guess, the experiment went well. So well that not only did I finish writing the book you're holding now, but some of these authors, who were so happy with their "cachet", ended up being clients of mine :)

---

[11] If you're a new writer, conditions will rarely be better than this.

CHAPTER 9

Reasons to self-publish

We've already looked at two good reasons to opt for self-publication:

1. It's much faster than doing it through a **real publishing house**.

2. It's much cheaper than doing it through a **fake publishing house**.

Maybe the question we should be asking ourselves is:

Why NOT self-publish?

If we went on the criteria of the writers I interviewed, there would be two main reasons for opting for a traditional publishing house:

1. Using a reputable publishing house **gives you more cachet**.

2. Self-publishing "professionally" **is not an easy task**.

To tell you the truth, I partially agree with them. Let me explain:

In terms of the first point, it's true that if you publish via an internationally renowned publishing house and it helps you to sell millions of copies worldwide, then yes, it gives you a certain cachet. Buuuut, if you pay several thousand dollars for the "co-publishing" place around the corner to "print" your book, I'm sorry to say that you're not an author with cachet, you're a *sucker*.

And when it comes to the second point, I agree once again. Self-publishing "professionally" is no mean feat. You only have to take a look at Amazon's catalog to see the aberrations that millions of indie authors upload to the platform showing off their Photoshop skills (or worse still, their Paint[12] skills!) or delighting readers with the wonders of Word's autocorrect. To tell you the truth, when I say I'm a self-published writer, I'm afraid people will associate me with these phenomena.

But what would you say if I told you you could self-publish your book with the same quality as a publishing house, but

---

[12] Microsoft Paint is a simple raster graphics editor that has been included with all versions of Microsoft Windows.

without having to learn graphic design or get a degree in philology – and that you could do it in less than a week?

Self-publishing a book is easy. As I said before, you can do it in under thirty minutes. Self-publishing a book **without it looking self-published** is a little trickier, but that's exactly what this second section is about!

If you follow the steps I'm going to give you in this guide, not only will you be able to self-publish with the same quality as a good publishing house – and achieve the same cachet or even more – you'll enjoy many of the hidden benefits that we self-published authors can obtain. These include the freedom to write what you want in your own words, not what your editor decides is more "suitable", and the control and flexibility to experiment and try new things when you – and you alone – decide, earning some good money along the way.

If all these reasons haven't convinced you and you still think you should go through a good publishing house, go ahead – but I advise you first to explore what you might achieve with "simple" self-publication. Once you've demonstrated that there are thousands of people prepared to buy your book, contact that company you're so interested in. This way, it will be you who negotiates the conditions.

CHAPTER 10

Why Amazon?

If you've read everything I've said and become an unconditional fan of the idea of publishing yourself, like I am, then you might be wondering:

Where do I publish my book?

There are many platforms you can self-publish on – some even have better conditions than Amazon (in terms of royalties). So why did I ultimately decide on Amazon, and why do I not hesitate in advising you to do the same?

There are several reasons that tipped the scales for me in favor of Bezos'[13] company, but there is one so blatant that it requires little explanation: Amazon is the world's biggest bookshop, so **it has the biggest database possible of readers for your book**. This means that **the potential for selling and earning**

---

[13] Jeff Preston Bezos is Amazon's founder and CEO.

money with your work is much greater on Amazon than on any other platform.

And if that's not enough: it also has the best control panel where you can closely follow everything that happens with your book, an exclusive platform where you can promote it, the option to publish both digital and physical books in dozens of different formats, an unparalleled delivery service (you'll quickly see your book delivered by smart drones in just a few hours or minutes), and more.

Okay, okay, so Amazon is the sh*t – but why not publish on the other platforms, too? I was mulling over this question for months. I eventually decided to postpone the idea indefinitely. There were two reasons why I made this decision:

1. Publishing on a platform requires just a few minutes, but **mastering a platform requires dedication**, so I ended up realizing it would be better to focus my energies on the nº1 platform, rather than spreading myself thin over others with less potential.

2. **With Amazon, exclusivity is rewarded**. If you promise not to publish your eBook anywhere else, Amazon offers you the chance to participate in its KDP Select program.

And this, my friends, is where it gets interesting.

CHAPTER 11

The KDP Select Program

KDP Select is a marketing program that involves giving Amazon exclusive rights to sell your book in digital format (you can still sell hard copies or audio versions wherever you want) for 90 days. At the end of this period, you can decide whether to continue with the program or not.

This option **is not selected** by default, so you have to check it when you publish. If you don't do it right then, you can sign up later from your book's homepage. It also renews automatically, so if you want to leave, you need to uncheck the option before the 90 days are up.

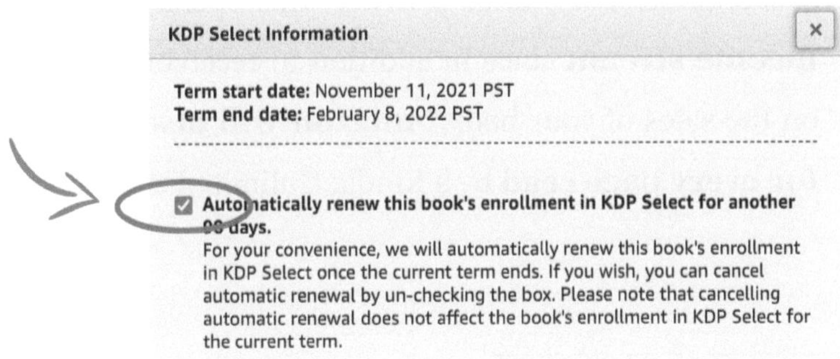

Where to find the KDP Select option.

Signing up to this program gives you a series of very interesting benefits and tools to help you succeed with your book – and Amazon is expanding and improving them all the time.

Using and analyzing these tools isn't something to worry about too much yet[14], since it's more about the marketing stage which we will look at in the next section, but I do think you should know **the 3 main benefits of KDP Select** when you are publishing your book and deciding whether or not to give Amazon that exclusivity:

1. **Better commission.** The first advantage of signing up to this program is that, in countries such as Japan, India, Mexico and Brazil, your royalties from sales of your eBook will go from **35% to 70%**.

2. **More income.** Every book registered with KDP Select is automatically included in **Kindle Unlimited**, a program with which customers can read as many books as they like and keep them indefinitely in return for a monthly subscription. For you as a writer, this opens up **a new income stream** since in addition to receiving royalties on the sales of your book, **Amazon will also pay you for every page read** by a Kindle Unlimited customer.

---

[14] If you're curious, you can find out more on their own website: *soykevinalbert.com/kdpselect*

3. **Greater visibility.** The evidence seems to suggest that Amazon gives "better treatment" – that is, more visibility – to KDP Select books. In addition, the pages read – alongside sales – will improve a book's ranking and see it climb the ladder in Amazon's library, which gives it even more visibility. It's a wonderful virtuous cycle: **more visibility, more sales; more sales, more visibility**.

CHAPTER 12

Layout: It's not enough to be an expert, you have to look like one

(Step 1)

Once your book has been through the editing process, you might think your manuscript is ready for publication. Wrong. What you say (your draft) and how you say it (your edited book) are equally important as the way you present it: that is, your book's layout.

This may seem superficial, and you might think all that matters to how your book is received is the content itself. I'm happy to tell you that this is not the case. Form matters – a lot! And I say I'm happy because layout is one of the simplest steps in the creation process, despite being the one lots of self-published authors skip out.

This is a great opportunity for writers to take things seriously, because even with a lower quality of content, your book will be better rated (get more stars) by readers, which will make it climb the ranks on Amazon, be more visible and get more sales than other books from the competition who didn't pay enough attention to this simple process.

What is layout?

Layout is the distribution of the elements of a given space on the page – in other words, the process of giving form to the book and getting it ready to be published.

During this process, you should pay attention to aspects such as margins, typography, line and paragraph spacing, style of titles and subtitles, page headers and footers, and so on.

Your aim with your layout is to give form coherence to the whole text: to choose a style and guarantee that it will be applied correctly throughout the entire book, so that the final result is conducive to comprehension and to make the experience as pleasant as possible for your readers.

Whose job is layout?

In general, if there are professionals specializing in a certain task – like there are for layout – I recommend outsourcing it. This is because if people do this task for a living, then no matter how simple it may seem to us, it must be trickier than it looks –

and I'm not going to recommend that you learn a new profession just in order to do something you might never need to do again in your life.

However, given that layout is a process that you need to go through several times in order to correct mistakes you find after your book has been published, as well as updating sections or expanding on the content, we're going to look at two options: outsourcing via Upwork, or DIY. This way, you can choose the option that adapts to your personal preferences and your particular situation.

1. Outsourcing: Upwork.

Just like you did when looking for an editor, all you have to do is publish your job offer (your book layout) following the steps indicated by the platform.

Disregard offers from less experienced professionals (those who have earned less than $12,000), as well as those with a success rate under 90%.

From the professionals still standing, look for those offering a reasonable rate (around $85 for either a physical or a digital version of your book) and prepared to help you with later corrections without charging you for the whole job again. This is an important point: if the freelancer you hire doesn't cover later modifications, or simply disappears from the platform, you will have to pay for the whole layout again. It happened to me, which is why, in this case, I broke my own rules and decided to learn to do it myself.

2. Do it yourself.

If you decide to DIY it, you'll need just two things: a Word template, and a little patience.

For the first of these, I recommend taking a look at Book Design Templates, a website specializing in book templates with over fifty different designs and prices varying between $29 and $59 per individual license:

soykevinalbert.com/bookdesigntemplates

All their templates are ready for editing, both in physical and in digital format. They also have some great tutorials to help you learn to do it easily, even if your Word knowledge is scant.

A GIFT FOR YOU

If you like the layout of this book, you can download my template through the following QR code:

CHAPTER 13

Cover:
Like it or not, your book will be judged by its cover

(Step 2)

Yes, as I explained in the first section, while your title is your n°1 secret to being **discovered** among the millions of books available on Amazon, without a doubt, your cover is the n°1 secret to being **chosen** from them.

Given that the cover is going to play such an important role in your book's success, **you need to take it seriously**. By this, I mean that you're not going to design it yourself, nor your brother-in-law who's great at drawing, nor your cousin with a degree in art... nor anyone who isn't a professional at designing book covers!

This part is important. In order to ensure we get a good book cover (one that sells), not only are we going to hire a professional in graphic design... **we're going to hire hundreds!**

Designer tournaments.

I really love tournaments and competitions, since I think they're a great way to get people to give it their all. That's why, in order to get the best cover possible for your book, you're going to pit dozens – or hundreds – of graphic designers against each other. To do this, you're going to use the platform Freelancer – although I personally don't like it as much as Upwork, it allows you to create contests or tournaments.

Why a contest?

Normally, to choose the best freelancer to work with, I recommend an active search like the ones I recommended performing through Upwork. However, on this occasion, in addition to looking for the best freelancer, **you're looking for ideas** – and the more, the merrier.

Paying a **good professional** $50 and asking them to suggest a hundred different ideas for your book cover is not realistic, no matter how cheap the cost of living is in their country. But you *can* ask for a different proposal from each of a hundred freelancers, and award a single $50 prize to the winning candidate.

How to create a contest.

Preparing a contest on Freelancer is easy. Go to the website *freelancer.com* and click "post a project" in the top right corner. Describe your project and indicate the skills that the participating freelancers will need to have (examples include graphic design, illustration, or Photoshop). Next, it will ask you how you want to create the job: either "post a project" or "start a contest". Once you have selected "start a contest", set your budget, how many days you want the competition to last, and whether you want the prize to be guaranteed[15].

To give you an idea of this, for the cover of this book, I set a $60 budget, allowed seven days for participation, and chose to guarantee the prize. With this configuration, I received 142 different pitches.

To increase your chances of getting the "perfect" book cover, one that you love, it's essential that you guide the participants in your contest. They need to know what you're looking for. This, along with a highly detailed description of the project, can be achieved with the following two tips:

1. Before posting your contest, do a search for covers on Amazon and Google and bookmark any that you really like. Choose book covers that are unrelated as well as related to your field. Once you have a good few (at least

---

[15] This means that you guarantee that even if no proposal really grabs you, you will choose one to award the prize to.

twenty), look for similarities between them. What is it that caught your eye? Why did you decide to bookmark them? You might realize that all books in your genre use the same color scheme, that you find minimalistic designs appealing, that you prefer those with illustrations, or something else.

When you upload your offer to Freelancer, include three to five of your favorite covers and indicate what you like best about them. Don't forget to specify that the final design needs to include a spine and back cover.

2. Check on your contest at least once a day and assign points to each proposal you receive. It's very important, if there's a cover you like much more than the others, that it has a higher points value than the others. If you have ten completely different proposals with the same points value, new candidates won't know what it was you liked or which elements to focus on in their designs. When it's clear that there is one idea you like more than the other, all participants will base themselves on that, trying to improve it. Similarly, if you haven't yet received one that grabs you, try not to award any of the designs five stars. This will ensure you keep receiving completely original pitches.

Prepare a survey.

As if the chance to create a contest wasn't already a little brutal, once the timeframe you set is up, you have the option to automatically schedule a survey so that your friends and acquaintances can help you choose the winning pitch.

This option is really interesting, and I recommend you always switch it on, even when you're clear on which design you like best. Imagine, for example, that you launch your survey and the proposal you had in mind gets almost no votes, while there's another one that it seems everyone loves. Wouldn't it make you reconsider? Remember that you're designing your cover to increase your book's chances of being chosen from Amazon's enormous online catalog, so if a significant proportion of people like the same proposal, surely it's at least worth considering.

Before you launch your survey, you need to wait for the timeframe you set to be up. Once the contest closes, you have up to four weeks to choose the winning proposal.

It's easy to create and share your survey. The platform will give you the option to select up to eight different pitches (or fewer, if you prefer). When you've selected the designs you want to include, Freelancer will give you some options for sharing them. I recommend you use the option to email your family and friends directly, as well as sharing a link to the survey on your social media. Once you've done this, wait five to seven days – and no longer – before looking over the results and making your final decision.

When you've chosen the winning proposal, you can award the prize to the design's creator – and, if necessary, ask them for a few adjustments or modifications before they deliver the finished product.

It's very important that you ensure the freelancer gives you the cover in an **editable format**, such as Photoshop or InDesign. This way, if you need to make any changes to the design in the future, any designer can help you to update it. In addition, you'll receive an **intellectual property contract** that guarantees that the work belongs to you.

And you're done!

If you've followed my steps, then in under fifteen days and for a measly $50, you can have a great book cover in your hands: designed by a professional, validated through a survey, and belonging completely to you. You're welcome.

Pro tip 1: To save time and unnecessary expenses adapting your cover to the final size of your book, upload the template Amazon gives you when you create your contest (along with the designs you include in your offer).

To get this template, go to: *kdp.amazon.com/cover-templates*, choose the same size you used for the book's layout, enter the number of pages in your document, select the paper color (white, cream or colored) and click "download cover template".

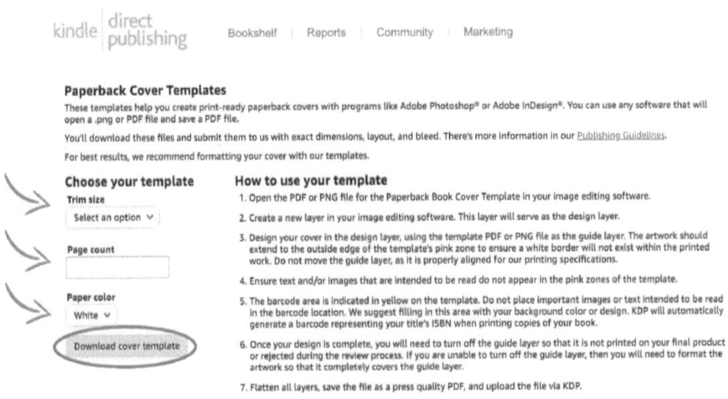

What you need to fill in to download your cover template.

Pro tip 2: For more objectivity in the results of your survey, before you choose the proposals you include in it, ensure they all have the same format: as simple as possible. Ideally, this will be a 2D design without additional decoration. If some of the designs you want to include in your survey were submitted in 3D or are simulated on top of a pretty desk or similar background, ask the creators to re-upload them in a simple format.

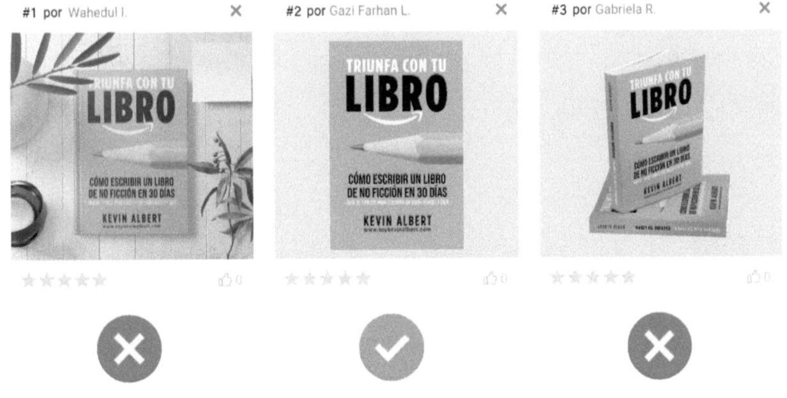

Left to right: design with decorations, 2D design, and 3D design.

CHAPTER 14

Description: Your best sales letter

(Step 3)

If you've managed to get potential readers to find your book, thanks to its title, and show an interest in it – thanks to its cover design – then it's time to sell it to them.

To do this, you're going to use a tool that's available to all authors on Amazon but that not many know how to make the most of: your book's description.

When we go to a bookshop in search of a new book and see one that catches our eye, what's the first thing we do? We turn it over and read the back cover. On Amazon, this is the role played by the description.

The mission of the description.

Since you can't be present each and every time someone is interested in your book in order to explain to them why they should choose you over the competition, it falls to your description to convince them. That is, it should play the role of a good commercial or sales letter.

How to write a perfectly irresistible description.

To write an irresistible description that's as appealing to Amazon itself as it is to your potential readers, you need just two things: using some simple copywriting skills (or persuasive writing), and applying a nice structure using HTML.

A) Copywriting.

Your book's description is not just there to tell the reader what the book is about (although that too). It's there to **persuade them to buy it**.

To achieve this, we're going to stick to 5 basic rules of copywriting:

1. Emotion.

In a non-fiction book, I consider that one of the best ways to start a description is by touching on your readers' sore points: that is, the problems they're facing, especially if you do so in question form.

For example, a good way of beginning the description for this book could be:

Have you spent years writing your book only to find no publishing house will touch it?

In addition, these first few words will be visible as soon as someone accesses the Amazon page for your book, without them needing to click on "read more" or scroll down. **Use them wisely**.

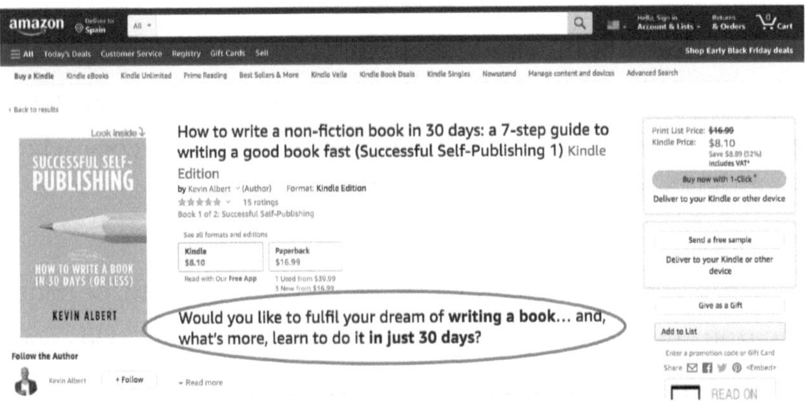

Visible part of the description on your book's product page.

2. Authority.

People look for others to trust in and follow their example. If you don't manage to portray yourself as an expert and/or to generate empathy with your readers, you're unlikely to sell your book.

Explain to the reader who you are to write this book. Why should they trust you? You may have a degree, a masters, a doctorate, you may have helped dozens or hundreds of people... or you may "simply" have been in their shoes and overcome the situation successfully.

3. Social proof.

Telling your readers why you're the best is all well and good, but if other people say it too, your credibility will shoot through the roof.

Specifically, being able to read what other customers of a book or other product think is one of the things that made Amazon the giant it is today. So, if you have a review from someone who's read your book, you can include it in your description.

If you don't have one yet, or if you receive new and/or better Amazon reviews, you can come back later and edit your description to add them or change the ones you included previously. Between three and five reviews in your description is more than enough.

You don't need to copy and paste the whole review: just write a summary or a standout phrase with the name of the person who wrote it. The more well-known they are, the more power their comments will have.

For example, I love to include my former teacher and fellow writer, José María Aznar, whenever I can. It's purely coincidental that he has the same name as the former prime minister of Spain... but people don't know that ;)

4. Benefits.

When a reader searches in the non-fiction section, they are normally trying to find a solution to a specific problem they have. Relieving that pain will be the main reason that will drive a user to buy your book – not necessarily your literary skills.

This means the benefits of your book can be the solution to your readers' problems. The reader must be able to see at a glance what benefits they will obtain from reading your book, so I recommend that you present them in a numbered list or with bullet points.

5. Call to action.

As I said before, you should view your description as a sales letter. As such, you should end it with a call to action, or CTA.

You need to finish your description with a phrase that tells the reader what they need to do after reading the description – that is, buy your book:

Stop talking about what you're going to do one day... AND JUST DO IT!

This is a great moment to touch on a sore point again:

If you let this chance go by, in a year's time you'll be regretting what you could have done and didn't.

Or add "urgency", another very potent copywriting resource, as long as it's true:

Don't hesitate! Introductory price ends this week.

Put your writing skills to work, and remember: don't sell, make them buy.

B) HTML.

Now that you have a perfectly optimized description thanks to some simple persuasive writing, it's time to dress it up. For this, we'll use HTML code, the language used on websites to format texts (among other things).

Why do this? Take a look.

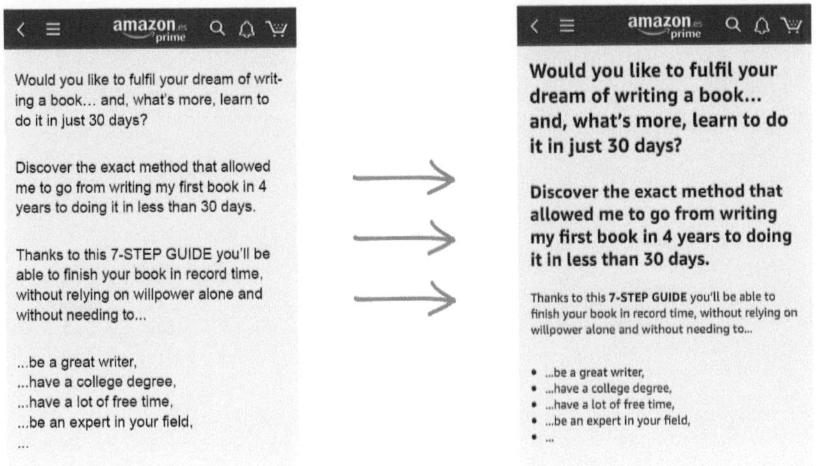

Description in plain text (left) and HTML (right).

As you can see, HTML enables you to change the size of the text, bold it, create lists with bullet points, and so on. All of this translates into better retention and better comprehension by your readers, which will undoubtedly have a positive effect on your sales.

And best of all is that you can do this without needing to learn absolutely anything about HTML coding, since while it was necessary for a long time to use external software to format descriptions, KDP finally decided to integrate this option and now we can do it directly from the extremely simple platform, as if it were a Word document:

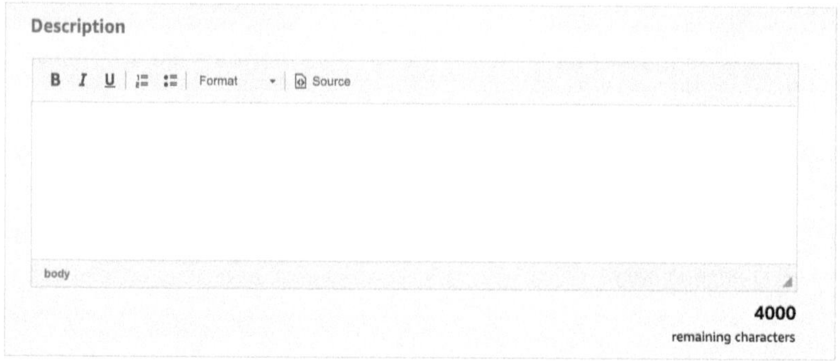

You now have an irresistible description that I'm sure will attract views... and sales!

Want more sales? Let's look at how to get them.

CHAPTER 15

Keywords:
How to ~~be found~~ get sold

(Step 4)

Whether you're an established writer or about to launch your first book, keywords are a fundamental aspect of your book's marketing strategy.

The **correct use** of keywords on Amazon will help your book be found and **bought** by hundreds of thousands of readers around the world. If you have, or are planning to write, an amazing book but don't know how to get Amazon to show it to the **right readers**, then keywords will be your best allies.

What are keywords?

When someone decides to buy a new book on Amazon, they go onto the website and type what they're looking for into the search bar. Amazon uses the characters the person typed to decide what books to show them. The words or phrases the person search are known as *keywords.*

How to find LUCRATIVE keywords.

Now you know what keywords are and why they're so important, but before you start choosing the best keywords for your book, first you need to know what makes a keyword **lucrative** – because being found isn't the same as selling.

For a keyword to be lucrative, it needs to fulfil 3 requirements:

1. Enough searches.
2. Not too much competition.
3. Readers prepared to pay for it!

1. How to find keywords with enough searches.

In order for your book to be discovered by the right readers, you need to know what terms your readers use when searching on Amazon. To achieve this, the first thing you need to do is put yourself in the shoes of your potential readers, and make a list of the terms you think they might use to search for your book. These are usually words or phrases associated with the topic of your work, solutions you're bringing, or results they'll obtain if they put into practice what they learn from your book.

For example, for the book you're reading right now, a key term related to the topic could be "publishing on Amazon" or "self-publishing on Amazon", while less obvious ones relating to the possible benefits they will obtain from reading it could be "passive income" or "extra money".

Once you have written this first list of keywords that you **think** your potential readers might use to find you, you need to **check** them.

To make sure your list is correct, use the **Amazon search bar** and start **slowly** typing each of the keywords or phrases you noted down. You need to type the characters one by one to see if Amazon suggests the term you were going to write before you finish writing it. If it does, that means that a significant number of people do, in fact, use these same words when searching.

To carry on with this example, let's imagine you thought that "publishing on Amazon" could be a good key phrase, so you go to the search bar and start typing the characters slowly. What would happen? As you can see in the below image, when you're up to "publishi...", Amazon will give you several suggestions relating to the keyword you were going to write.

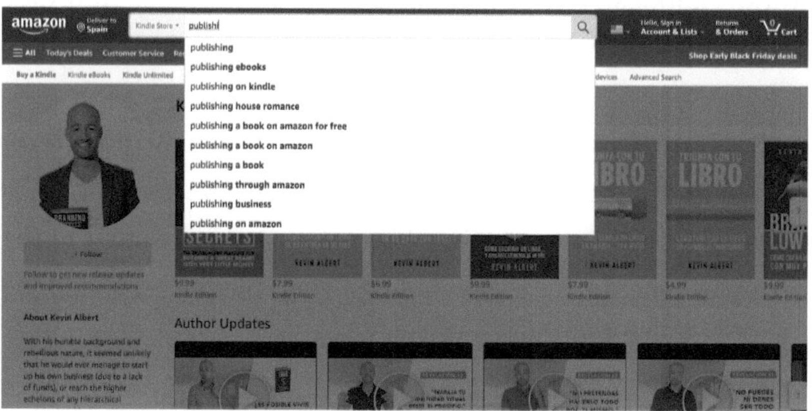

Amazon's predictive search function.

What conclusions can you draw from this? Firstly, that "publishing on Amazon" is indeed a key phrase that a significant number of people search for on Amazon – if it weren't, it wouldn't suggest it to us. And secondly, that "publishing a book" has more searches.

Amazon doesn't tell you how many people searched for a given word, but it does order the results by number of searches. This means that before you analyze both keywords in depth, it looks like "publishing a book" is a better option (with more searches) than "publishing on Amazon". But as they both appeared as suggestions, note them both down on your list for the second part of the analysis.

If any of the words you wrote down don't appear as suggestions when you start typing them into Amazon, you can deduce that they don't get many searches and discard them.

Things to bear in mind:

1. Make sure you're using your browser's incognito mode; if you don't, the results will be affected by your previous searches and they won't be reliable.

   To do this, just open the application bar in the browser you're using (Safari, Chrome, Firefox, or others) and select "New incognito [or private] window".

2. Select "Kindle Store" in Amazon's search bar before beginning your research. You're interested in finding out which words are popular in your section (books or eBooks), not on all of Amazon. By default, it will be set to "All Departments".

Search bar set to Kindle Store.

3. Do your research in the specific marketplace you're interested in (.com, .uk, .es, etc.), since these are different markets and their suggested terms may vary.

Tip: once you've chosen your keywords or phrases, type them into Amazon again and add one letter of the alphabet at a time. Start with A and work your way through to Z.

Example:

- Publishing on Amazon a
- Publishing on Amazon b
- Publishing on Amazon c
- Etc.

Look at the suggestions Amazon gives you. See anything good?

This is a great way to find some good (and lucrative) keywords that might never have occurred to you otherwise. In addition, if Amazon suggests them to you, it means they get a significant volume of searches.

2. How to know which keywords have the least competition.

Knowing which keywords are the most searched-for is very important, but not if you don't know the competition you face for each of them, you'll be making decisions blind.

Luckily, there is a very simple strategy you can use to ascertain the level of competition. All you have to do, while following the considerations I mentioned above, is type your key terms into Amazon's search bar and note down how many results you get.

Number of results for the search term "publishing a book".

If you compare the two keywords in the previous point, you get the following results:

- Publishing a book: 40,000 results.
- Publishing on Amazon: 60,000 results.

Just by using this rudimentary system, we've discovered that "publishing a book", not only has more searches than our original key term ("publishing on Amazon"), but it also has less competition. *BOOM*!

You now have a list of keywords with a significant number of searches and you've ordered them according to their levels of competition. All that's left is to figure out which keywords have the most potential to generate sales.

3. How to find keywords readers will pay for.

Now we know which keywords from our list are most searched by readers, and which have less competition. Fantastic. But what use is this if it doesn't translate into sales?

This step is the most labor-intensive, but it's simple and undoubtedly the most important. To find out the sales potential of a keyword:

a) Type it into Amazon's search bar, bearing in mind the aforementioned considerations.

b) Note down the position in Amazon's ranking of the first ten books your search brings up. To find this position, you need to click on the book in question and scroll down to "product details". Here, you'll see the ranking for that book in its specific categories and in the **general classification of Amazon's bestsellers, or ABSR**[16]. This last figure is the one we're looking for.

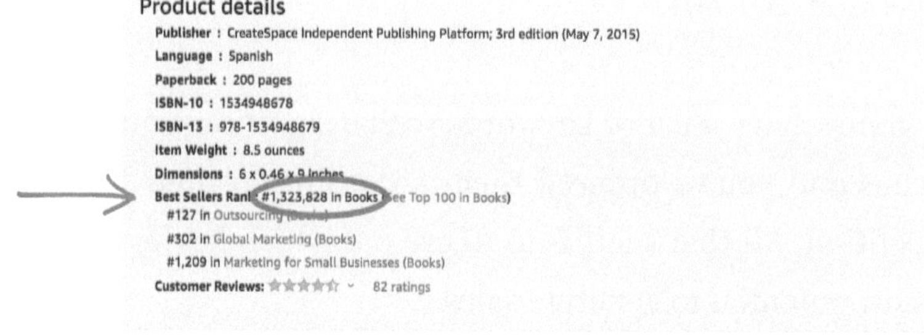

Where to find the general classification of bestsellers on Amazon.

c) Add up the positions of these books, and divide the resulting number by 10.

---

[16] Amazon Bestseller Rank.

Compare this result for the different keywords you're analyzing. Those with a lower number will have the greatest sales potential.

Pro tip: if you want to make this process more efficient and you're interested in knowing, among other things, how much your competition earns from their books (I'm nosy like that), I highly recommend the tool Publisher Rocket:

soykevinalbert.com/rocket

So, you have your lucrative keywords. Now what?

Now, it's time to use these keywords to show Amazon that your book deserves to be shown to your potential readers when they search... and when they don't!

To do this, try to include them, **without sounding robotic**, in your book's title and/or subtitle, in its description, and – of course – in the section reserved specifically for keywords.

When you're uploading your book to KDP, you'll find a space where you can enter up to seven keywords. If you did your homework properly, this section has tremendous value potential. Don't squander it.

CHAPTER 16

Categories: Improve your ranking and sell more books

(Step 5)

The categories you choose for your book when you upload it to KDP will have a direct impact on its potential to turn you into a bestselling author. There's no easier way to make your book a super-seller than by choosing your categories carefully. Similarly, if you choose the wrong categories, your chances of achieving this may vanish completely.

In the Amazon universe, it's much better to be a big fish in a little pond than a small fish in the Pacific. The good news is that Amazon's algorithm, once you've conquered the small pond, will push you into the Pacific, too.

How important is it to be an Amazon bestseller?

Being an Amazon bestseller is not just an ego thing – it will **help you sell more books**. There are several factors that make this possible:

- **Amazon's algorithm itself** will give your book more exposure purely because it occupies the upper positions in a category.

- **Searches by category** by many readers will enable your book to be discovered by people who would not have otherwise found you.

- The **bestseller badge** Amazon will automatically add to your book listing once you have reached top position in a category will increase your views-to-sales conversion ratio. In other words, for the same number of views of your book, you will sell more copies of it.

I'm sure you've heard that it's songs played on the radio that become hits and not the other way around (like you'd think it would be). Well, something similar happens with Amazon – but unlike in the music industry, you don't have to pay for it or do anybody any little favors.

Being a bestseller will help you sell more books, and vice versa.

What do you need to become a bestseller in an Amazon category?

First of all, it's fundamental that you properly understand what the **ABSR** is. This number (which we already used in the previous chapter to find the most lucrative keywords) depends on the sales and/or downloads of a book over a given time period, compared to other books on Amazon The more sales/downloads, the lower the ABSR.

Let's imagine that, at a certain point, your book has an ABSR of 100. This means that there are only 99 other books on all of Amazon that are selling more than yours. If your ABSR was 1000, there would currently be 999 books selling better than yours, and so on and so forth.

So, if you have the lowest ABSR of all the books in a given category, you would be n°1 in that category. It's that simple.

Example: if you choose a category where the n°1 has an ABSR of 500, then to reach first place, your book will need an ABSR of 499 or less.

This means that the categories you choose when uploading your book to KDP have a direct impact on your chancing of becoming a bestselling author.

How to find the best categories.

To find the most suitable categories with the most potential for turning your work into a bestseller, just follow three simple steps:

1. Find the possible categories for your book.

To find these possible categories, head to the "Product details" section of similar books to yours (they may be in direct competition with you or not) and note down the categories these appear under. You'll see that each book is included in two or three different categories.

Location of categories under "Product details".

Try to make a list of at least 5 possible categories.

2. Find out the nº1 book in each category.

Now that you have your list of possible categories, it's time to find out which have the best chance of turning your book into a bestseller.

To do this, first go to the list of the bestselling books in each of these categories by clicking on the name of each category in the "Product details" section of each book you're researching.

Once you're in, click on the nº1 book for each of these categories and note down its ABSR. This is the ABSR you'll have to beat in order to become a bestseller in that category. The higher the ABSR, the easier you'll find it to reach nº1.

Pro tip: If you use Publisher Rocket, then in addition to saving yourself hours of work, you can find out the number of books you need to sell in twenty-four hours in order to reach first place in each category.

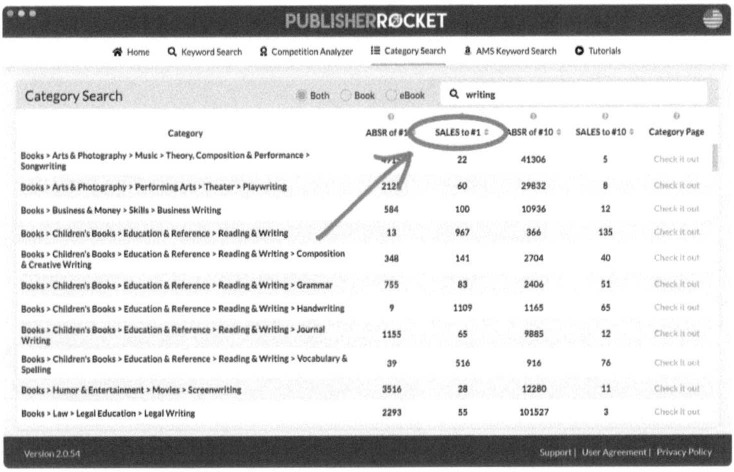

PUBLISHERROCKET

Home | Keyword Search | Competition Analyzer | Category Search | AMS Keyword Search | Tutorials

Category Search — Both / Book / eBook — writing

Category	ABSR of #1	SALES to #1	ABSR of #10	SALES to #10	Category Page
Books > Arts & Photography > Music > Theory, Composition & Performance > Songwriting	[illegible]	22	41306	5	Check it out
Books > Arts & Photography > Performing Arts > Theater > Playwriting	[illegible]	60	29832	8	Check it out
Books > Business & Money > Skills > Business Writing	584	100	10936	12	Check it out
Books > Children's Books > Education & Reference > Reading & Writing	13	967	366	135	Check it out
Books > Children's Books > Education & Reference > Reading & Writing > Composition & Creative Writing	348	141	2704	40	Check it out
Books > Children's Books > Education & Reference > Reading & Writing > Grammar	755	83	2406	51	Check it out
Books > Children's Books > Education & Reference > Reading & Writing > Handwriting	9	1109	1165	65	Check it out
Books > Children's Books > Education & Reference > Reading & Writing > Journal Writing	1155	65	9885	12	Check it out
Books > Children's Books > Education & Reference > Reading & Writing > Vocabulary & Spelling	39	516	916	76	Check it out
Books > Humor & Entertainment > Movies > Screenwriting	3516	28	12280	11	Check it out
Books > Law > Legal Education > Legal Writing	2293	55	101527	3	Check it out

Version 2.0.54 — Support | User Agreement | Privacy Policy

And that's it. With this small research you've just conducted, you now know which categories are the most suitable for your book's topic and, most importantly, which ones have the best chances of boosting you to become a bestseller author: those with a higher ABSR.

Now you just need to choose your three favorites and add them in the appropriate section when you upload your book to KDP.

CHAPTER 17

Pricing: Strategies and promotions

(Step 6)

You're almost there. The last section you will have to fill out when uploading your book to KDP is your book's price. Because unlike what happens when you work through a publishing house, on Amazon the price is set by you.

Is this a good thing? Very.

But before moving onto the technical aspects of this, let me tell you a story:

> My cousin once asked me if I could meet with a friend of his who was a neurosurgeon and writer. He told me that he had published his first book through a publishing house, but he was planning to publish his second through Amazon and didn't know whether to do it or whether it was a good idea. Of

course, I told him I was happy to have a coffee with him and help him as much as I could.

A few days later, he called me and we met at one of my favorite cafes (the kind I write in). To my surprise, I had taken more time learning about him and his book than he had about me.

The first thing he said to me when we sat down was: "so, your cousin tells me you have a book on Amazon". Things weren't looking good.

He admitted to me – although I already knew it – that his book actually hadn't been published through a publishing house, but rather he had spent over $7000 on the *printing scam*, and only sold around a hundred copies. This is the only reason he had wanted to talk to me: my cousin had told him I had published "safely", without spending a lot of money, and he was going to publish his new book himself whatever it took (although he couldn't imagine making any profit from it) and wanted to know if it was possible to save a few bucks.

Based on this, where the only thing this person knew about me was that I had published through Amazon without investing much, my recommendations weren't very useful – in his eyes, I had no authority. It was more like a meeting between two friends defending their respective points of view than it was a free advice session. Fun, sure, but not awfully valuable.

In the end, I decided to relax and enjoy my coffee while having a chat with an interesting person. I wasn't there to prove myself, and my ego was perfectly comfortable. However, not long before we said goodbye, the topic of pricing came up and things changed. When we had already asked for the check, he suddenly asked me:

- Just out of interest, how much are you selling your book for?
- Well, right now, the Kindle version is at $10, and the paperback at $30.
- What?! $30?! How many pages is your book?!
- Around 170, if I remember correctly.
- Listen, let me tell you something: my book has over 400 pages and I'm selling it at $14.99, and I've barely sold a hundred copies in over three years. At your prices, you're not going to sell at all.

It's true that I wasn't there to prove anything to anyone, but since the topic had come up... telling him about my sales was highly satisfying :)

His expression was incredulous, and he began to debate (mostly with himself) and explain "to me" why "I" couldn't be selling that many books while simultaneously asking me how I had managed it (?!).

This neurosurgeon-slash-writer was trying nervously to tell me that a book is sold by weight (no doubt that's what the "publishing house" told him), so mine "needed" to be a lot cheaper if I wanted to sell it.

I tried to explain the **concept of value** to him in a few different ways, but there was no telling him. Eventually, I took a napkin from the dispenser (the kind you need twenty-three of to get your hands clean), pretended I was writing something on it, folded it up and slid it across the table, telling him:

- Imagine that on this napkin is written the formula that enables you to turn water into gold. How much would you pay me for it?
- Everything I had (he answered pretty quickly).
- Would you pay me $30?
- I'd give you my house for it.
- But this napkin barely weighs anything.

I don't think he liked my napkin metaphor much, but it got my point across, because the next thing he said was "for $30, you're not going to sell many books", before paying the check at the counter, saying goodbye, and never contacting me again.

Am I telling you this story so that you set any price for your book that you like, no matter what the rest of the market is doing?

No.

I just want you to understand that the price you set for your book needs to have a reason behind it, and that – especially if we're talking about a non-fiction book – it shouldn't be based on its weight.

How to price your book.

Just like with the writing process itself, setting a price for your work is half art, half science. The aspects to bear in mind when finding the perfect amount are myriad, but let's look at what I consider to be the **3 most important**:

1. Your objectives.

The first step to finding the right price is to ask yourself what the objective of your book is:

a) You may see your book as an investment or mini-business in itself, and want to get the most profits possible from sales – in which case, you're looking at finding the best price/sales/income relationship.

That means, generally and logically speaking, the higher the price, the fewer sales, and the lower the price the more sales. This is clear, but what price/sales relationship will give us the most income at the end of each month?

b) Alternatively, you may see your book as a way to get your message across and help as many people as you can, without minding what profit you make from selling it. If this is you, it's logical that the cheaper your book is, the more people you'll be able to reach.

   WARNING: Someone who buys your book just because it's cheap, as an impulse buy, may not end up reading it. In addition, a low price can suggest low quality, which could be reflected in your reviews and negatively impact on your sales in the long term.

c) It's likely that your objective for your book is somewhere in between. You may want to reach as many people as possible without caring about profits from direct sales of your book... but you're also hoping to get some profits, or to use your book as a way to get customers to buy other products or services from you later. You may want to use your book as a kind of resumé to get a new job, or a promotion at your current company. The possibilities are endless; **what matters is that you're clear on your objective**.

2. The competition.

Taking a look at your competition is the fastest way to get an idea of the prices other books in your category sell for. This is a great starting point to avoid aiming too high or too low.

But don't get obsessed with this, either. It's just a reference point. I have had customers terrified to set the same price as well-known authors or books with many more pages than their own, and ending up setting their prices purely based on this criterion, with no real strategy in mind. **You have to get rid of that fear**.

Amazon has democratized both publishing and selling books: not only can you publish your book just the same as your favorite authors... you can get ahead of them and beat their sales figures!

Unlike what has always happened in traditional bookshops, where the best spot (the shiny, well-lit shelf just in front of the entrance, packed from top to bottom with copies of the same book) was reserved for the big author that a big publishing house decided to promote that month, with Amazon that spot is just the first in the list when a reader searches for something (whether through keywords or by category) and **it's reserved for... the best book**. Not for the best-known author, or the publishing house that paid to be there. If your book is the best, it doesn't matter if it's the first time you've ever published anything, or if you're not even a household name in your own house – **it will appear at the top of the list**. In everyone's eyeline.

And how do Amazon decide who is the best? It's simple: **with stars**. This is how Amazon readers show their satisfaction rating. The more stars, the happier they are, with five being the maximum.

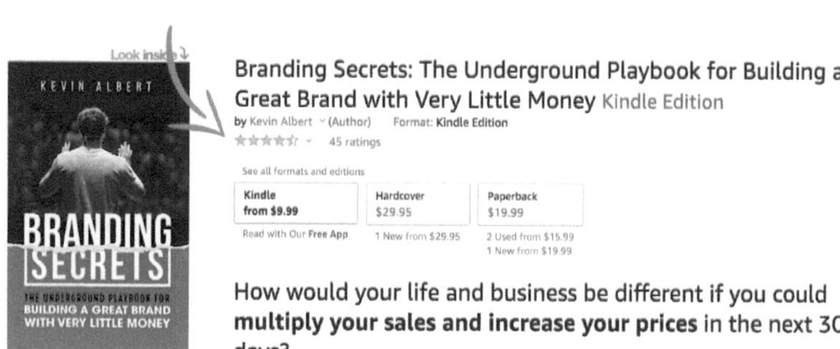

Location of the star rating on the product page.

This will also work in your favor as a new author in terms of expectations. When we watch a movie we have high expectations for, because it contains our favorite actor, for example, it's easier for us to be disappointed. However, the first time we "risk" investing our money in a movie or book by an unknown writer, we have no expectations yet and it's less likely we'll be disappointed. On top of that, readers seem to be more permissive in terms of print quality or minor grammatical errors, for example, with self-published authors than with big publishing houses, from whom they demand near perfection.

If you're still worried about pricing your book the same as "big name writers", remember that I didn't set the price of my first book the same as the competition – I set it at exactly double! $10 for the Kindle version, $30 for the paperback.

While risky, there was a reason for this strategy. Firstly, I wanted to differentiate myself, as a book by an unknown author that's double the price of books by well-known author will inevitably make readers wonder: "what the hell is up with this book?" (This is why it's important to have good reviews). Secondly, I knew my book was worthwhile in comparison with other branding books on the market, which seem only to talk about companies the size of Coca-Cola.

Careful! If you decide to set a higher price than your competition in order to increase your book's perceived value, make sure its real value doesn't disappoint your readers.

In any case, the most-used strategy in relation to the competition's prices, which will also help you sleep at night (I think I like danger too much), is to launch your book at a lower price and then increase it to match the competition when you reach a certain number of reasonable reviews (at least half those of the competition).

3. The value you add.

As I explained to my cousin's friend, when it comes to pricing your book, one factor you should bear in mind – especially for non-fiction – is the value it adds for readers.

Logic, and Amazon statistics, indicate that we are prepared to pay more money for a non-fiction book than a fiction one. In other words: we will pay more to solve a problem than we will to be entertained.

So, before you set a price for your book, ask yourself: "what can my book do for my readers? Are there any other books on the market that do the same thing?". I don't mean that your book has to present a completely original solution or idea. Sometimes, saying the same thing from a different perspective or with a better structure can in itself be priceless.

So, does this mean that if your book solves some existential problem, you can set whatever price you want for it? No. What it means is that you can set a "high" price in relation to your competition.

Although I would happily pay over a thousand dollars for some of the books on my own shelf (they've earned me a lot more than that), if you really want to sell, you need to set a "book price". As high as you want, but appropriate for a book.

Even if you know the secret to eating without getting fat – something millions of people would give their right arm for – the price of your book needs to meet the expected standards. My recommendation in this case would probably be to use your work to position yourself as an expert and obtain clients for personal consulting or one of your conferences later on – then, you really can charge as much as you want. It's sad that it has to be that way, but it's what we're used to.

I have been invited to conferences costing over $3000 and never learned anything more than I already knew from the book by the author giving the talk, which cost less than $30.

Psychological strategies.

Now, let's look at two simple psychological and logical strategies that will help you sell more books.

a) The magic of the .99

Like it or not, this crude strategy invented in the 19th century still has a significant impact on our shopping habits.

If you price your book at $5, for example, you'll sell fewer than if you set it at $4.99. It's that simple. From a logical point of view, this makes no sense: $4.99 is only one cent less than $5, which doesn't constitute any savings for the buyer. But our brains interpret it differently.

Since we read from left to right, our brain – which loves to simplify things – focuses on the number before the dot. This means that when the price starts with a 4, our brain files it under

"4" (4 dollars and something), but if the price starts with a 5, we file it under "5".

Another hypothesis says that prices that end in .99 are associated with discounts or promotions. And when we think we're getting a deal, we're more likely to buy it right away.

Pro tip: when you've finally decided on a price for your book and you enter it into the corresponding field on KDP, don't make the mistake of letting the platform calculate the same price for the rest of your markets as your main market (which you choose). If, for example, you decided to use the .99 strategy, apply it manually to all available markets. It will take you less than a minute and make a big difference over the course of a year.

b) Multiprices.

If you have written, or plan to write, more than one book, you may think it's a good idea to set the same price for all of them (the price that worked best for you elsewhere) – especially if they have the same theme and similar lengths. This will end up having a negative impact on your sales.

Using what's known as multiple pricing will help you benefit from different customers' **value perception**. For example, if you price one book at $11.99 and another at $19.99, thanks to the price comparison that happens subconsciously in consumers' heads, you will attract both readers looking for a good deal and readers who prefer the premium option.

Experiment.

One of the good things about Amazon is that you can change the price of your book whenever you want, as often as you want.

You can start by pricing your work following the recommendations I've given you in this chapter, or you can do the total opposite and ignore my tips entirely. In the end, there is no perfect price, and no matter what I tell you or how many successful cases I show you, nothing can replace the power of experimentation.

Are you someone who thinks the price of your book should be based on the number of pages or words it has? Go ahead. Amazon itself will show you price tables according to this criterion.

Have you read somewhere that the eBook should cost half the physical version? Try it out.

Or do you think that if you price them similarly, then sales of your paperback will go through the roof? Give it a go and see what happens.

Allow yourself to try things, and don't be afraid of making mistakes. Worst case scenario, you'll have a month of slower sales (or profits), and the next month[17] you can try a different combination of prices (Kindle and paperback) that worked well for you before, or try something totally new.

---

[17] I recommend that each test lasts at least 30 days so you can draw solid conclusions from it.

Can I tell you a secret? I realized that every time I make a small modification on KDP, whether it's to fix an error in the description, upload a new cover, or change the price of one of my books, my sales go up that week. Don't ask me why, but **Amazon's algorithm likes change**. If that doesn't encourage you to experiment, I don't know what will.

Promotions.

Signing up to the KDP program will enable you to run two kinds of promotion on your book, totally free: **Kindle Countdown Deals,** and **free book promotions**.

To start a promotion, just click "promote and advertise" from your KDP dashboard, and once you're in, select one of the above two options.

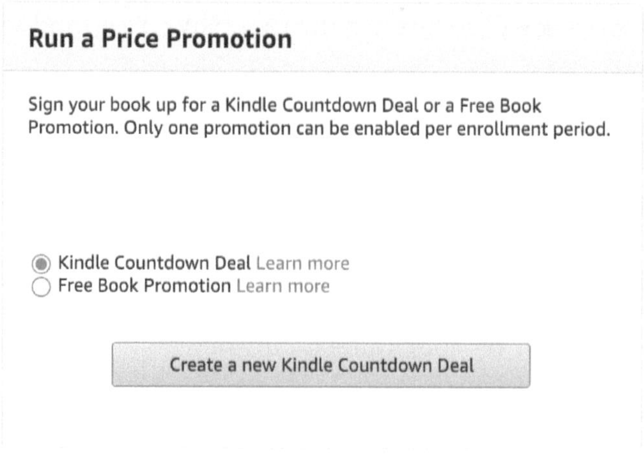

Run a Price Promotion

Sign your book up for a Kindle Countdown Deal or a Free Book Promotion. Only one promotion can be enabled per enrollment period.

Kindle Countdown Deal Learn more
Free Book Promotion Learn more

Create a new Kindle Countdown Deal

KDP Select promotion options.

1. Kindle Countdown Deals.

This type of promotion will allow you to set a lower price for your book for a limited period. Customers will be able to see its usual price alongside the promotional price on the book details page, as well as a clock showing the time remaining at the promotional price.

All you have to do is select a **start** and **finish date** (with a maximum period of seven days), the **number of price increases** (with a maximum of five) and the **starting price**.

Imagine you have a Kindle book with a normal price of $9.99 and you decide to run this promotion from Monday to Friday, with a starting price of $1.99. With this configuration, Amazon will show your book at $1.99 for 37 hours and at $5.99 for the remaining 38 hours, before returning it to its original price of $9.99.

Increments		Duration	Price	% Discount
1	21 junio 2020 at 8:00 (PDT)	37h	$1.99	81%
2	22 junio 2020 at 21:00 (PDT)	37h	$3.99	61%
3	24 junio 2020 at 10:00 (PDT)	38h	$5.99	41%
Fin	26 junio 2020 at 0:00 (PDT)		$9.99	

Example of a configuration with Kindle Countdown Deals.

The idea is to motivate people to buy with the incentive that, if they leave it till later, the book will be more expensive. The bigger the discount, the more motivating it is.

This type of promotion has **two main advantages**:

- **You maintain your royalties.** You will receive royalties according to your normal rate, applied to the promotional price. So, if you're signed up to the 70% royalties option, you'll get 70% even if the price is less than $2.99.
- **More sales,** both because of the incentive of seeing a reduced price and a countdown timer, and because of the greater visibility you will get by including your book in an additional category: "Featured Kindle Countdown Deals".

Requirements for participating in Kindle Countdown Deals:

- The eBook must be signed up to KDP Select for at least 30 days before you launch the promotion.
- The price must have remained the same for those 30 days, and for 14 days following the end of the promotion.
- The minimum discount is $1 on Amazon.com and £1 on *Amazon.co.uk* (the only two markets on which you can run this promotion currently).
- However long you set the time period for, this will count as a complete promotion (you can't divide the promotion between separate time periods).
- You haven't run another KDP Select promotion for that eBook. You can only schedule one promotion (free book or

Kindle Countdown Deals) per inscription period with KDP Select (90 days).

- Kindle Countdown Deals must be scheduled at least 24 hours before their start date. For example, for the promotion to begin on January 10th, you can schedule it at any point prior to January 8th.
- The Kindle Countdown Deals promotion will end a maximum of 14 days before your KDP Select sign-up period ends. If you renew your book with KDP Select for another 90 days, your Kindle Countdown Deals promotion can end on the last day of your current period with KDP Select.

2. Free book promotions.

This type of promotion enables you to offer your book for free for 5 days (consecutive or alternating) for each sign-up period with KDP Select (90 days). And, unlike Kindle Countdown Deals, **it is not limited** to Amazon.com and Amazon.co.uk.

The best thing to do if you decide to use this promotion is to run the 5 days consecutively, starting on Sunday and ending on Thursday, since these are the days of the week with the most sales.

A few years ago, this promotion gave great results because during the days for which people could get the book for free, you would get a lot of downloads (especially if used in conjunction with other strategies), which sent your book up the **free books ranking.** When the promotional period was over, the rank you achieved on this list would help you move up the **paid books ranking** (the one we're interested in). Nowadays, you don't get this transfer of positions between the two lists, so this option is used less widely – although it can still be helpful in certain specific cases:

- Authors publishing a book for the first time, with no established target market. This can be a good way to get a significant number of downloads and make yourself known, as well as obtaining some early reviews.

- Authors who aren't looking to make money from their book. A free book will, without a doubt, be downloaded by more people. But be careful – more downloads doesn't necessarily mean more readers. People who only download a book because it's free tend to accumulate hundreds of books they never get round to reading.

- Authors planning to turn their books into series. It can be a good idea to offer the first book for free as a hook to get more sales on your other books later.

CHAPTER 18

Upload your book to Amazon

If you've followed the 7 steps in this section, you have all the elements you need ready to upload your book to KDP.

To begin, all you need to do is create an account. Go to *kdp.amazon.com*, click "Sign in" and enter your Amazon details, or click "Sign up" and create a new account. Fill in your personal and financial details and tell them the bank account you want Amazon to pay your royalties into (it's much better than getting a check).

All that's left is to upload your book. Choose the format you want to start with —Kindle, Paperback or Hardcover— and check the corresponding box.

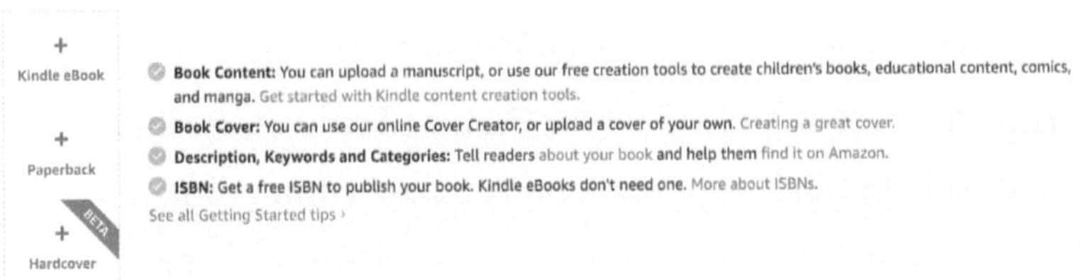

KDP user panel.

You'll see that the details to fill in are classed into three main sections: details, content and book price. It's all very simple. There are only five things that tend to generate doubts the first time you upload a book (if you have any others, don't hesitate to ask me):

1. **Publishing rights**. Check the first option: «I own the copyright and I hold the necessary publishing rights».

2. **Physical ISBN**. Click «Assign me a free KDP ISBN».

3. **Territories**. Select «All territories».

4. **Digital Rights Management (DRM)**. I recommend you don't enable this, as it's been proven that books with DRM don't sell as well.

5. **Signing up to KDP Select**. Of course, I recommend signing up, since – as I mentioned before – it's given me better results in my experiments (more profits), but it's ultimately a personal decision.

And that's it!

You will have realized by now that, as I said at the start of this section, self-publishing a book on Amazon (uploading it to KDP) takes no more than thirty minutes, but self-publishing a book on Amazon **properly and with the best chances of success** requires a little more preparation in order to correctly organize each of the sections we've gone through.

I hope I've conveyed the importance of taking care over each of these 7 steps and that I have explained them clearly and simply, so that you too can achieve, without needing a publishing house...

Successful self-publishing!

SELL YOUR BOOK

- HOW TO SELL A BOOK ON AMAZON AND LIVE OFF IT! -

The trouble with the rat race is that even if you win, you're still a rat.

— LILY TOMLIN

Introduction

Having dedicated four years of my life to writing my first book and another half a year to publishing it, the moment of truth had arrived. Would all the blood, sweat and tears bear fruit and turn into sales?

I knew that the quality of my book was excellent, both inside – I was solving a latent problem – and outside: the cover, layout, editing, and so on had all been performed by professional experts.

I also knew that I would undoubtedly become a bestselling author, because I had done my research into how to launch a book successfully on Amazon.

But despite all this, the week of publication, when things were going great, I remember remarking to a fellow entrepreneur: "I would love for the book to bring in a hundred dollars a month."

A hundred dollars?!

Knowing that the book I had in my hands was amazing, and that the launch was going to be spectacular... why was I happy to settle for a hundred measly dollars a month? Well, it's because I know the online world very well.

There are some incredible products online that aren't known and don't sell because they are poorly marketed, and there are mediocre products that generate millions (Hawkers sunglasses, for example) because they have good marketing strategies.

Of course, my economic outlook would have been very different had I been prepared to work for my book (create a blog or podcast, deliver conferences, invest in marketing, and so on), but I already had a job that took up all of my time and **what I wanted was for the book to work for me, not the other way around.** I wanted a **100% passive extra income.**

Fortunately, after launching and reaching the "bestseller" position in several Amazon categories, my book continued to sell relatively well and **profits were at around $230 a month**: three times what I had signed up for without hesitating a few months previously.

I was more than happy. A book written out of sheer pig-headedness had shot to the upper ranks on Amazon, ahead of internationally renowned authors. It had improved my personal brand beyond belief – so I was receiving job offers that had been unthinkable before – and I was pocketing over $2000 a year for my vacations.

What more could I want?

I had already achieved much more than what dozens of books on *how to successfully self-publish your book on Amazon* promise.

But a year later, something happened that changed everything: my father retired.

Like many other people his age, my father entered the world of work at a very young age – twelve – and he had not had a single sick day in over fifty years of work, nor had he ever taken more than two weeks' leave in one go. Can you imagine my indignation when I found out that, despite it all, his pension was going to be less than $1000 a month?

$1000 a month after a lifetime of hard graft!

I was incensed, so I decided to utilize my rage constructively.

That was when I decided to find a way for anyone who wrote a book to create a passive income of at least $1000 a month in under a year – not fifty-four years, like my dad.

As a result of this personal mission, involving three years of research and an investment of over $5000 in various training courses, I finally found **a system that enables both writers and non-writers to generate passive income of at least $1000 a month with a single non-fiction book**.

The objective of this book is to allow you to ~~create a decent retirement pension in under a year~~ ESCAPE THE SYSTEM.

You heard right. My main aim when writing these words, as I said at the start of this book, is to **change the world**. I'm sure you can think of other - maybe even better - ways to do it, but without a doubt **helping you to escape the system or "rat race"** is a great way to do it.

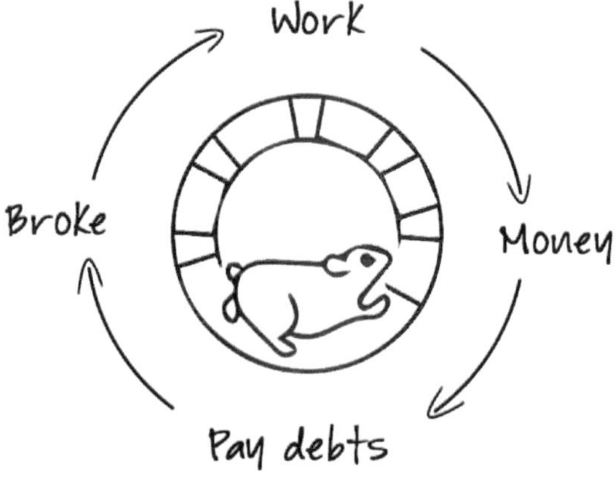

The rat race.

If you know me personally or follow me on social media, I'm sure you know that in addition to writing, I have my fingers in a lot of other pies: most of them projects with the potential to generate much more income than a book can. So...

Why a book?

Why don't I teach you another kind of business that can generate $10,000 or $100,000 a month?

1. A book has enough potential.

You might think $1000 a month is a tiny amount (I do), but that's the pension my father was left with after a lifetime of work.

The objective of this guide is to teach you how to match or beat that figure in under a year, and a book has enough potential to do so.

2. You don't need to invest.

I can't think of any other business where you can invest less than $180 (for the editing, cover and layout) and obtain an income of over $1000 a month.

3. Time.

Getting a retirement pension of $1000 a month may require over fifty years of total dedication. With a book, you can achieve that in under a year with just a few hours' work a week.

4. 100% passive.

Once your book is out there, the income will roll in each month without you having to do anything.

5. 0% risk.

Unlike other types of business, you don't have to quit your day job, risk it all and scrape by until your new project works – if it does at all!

6. You don't need to create a website.

One of the main advantages of online business is that you don't have to rent a physical space in order to operate; a good website is enough.

If you sell your book on Amazon, you don't even need to do that; Amazon will be your website, and it's an amazing one.

7. You don't need to learn about marketing.

In order to sell any product online (or offline), you have to apply a marketing strategy. Whether you decide to outsource or opt for learning to do it yourself, you will have to create a minimum viable **sales funnel**. That means you will need to **attract** users to your product, **convert** those users into leads (potential customers), and **sell them** your product.

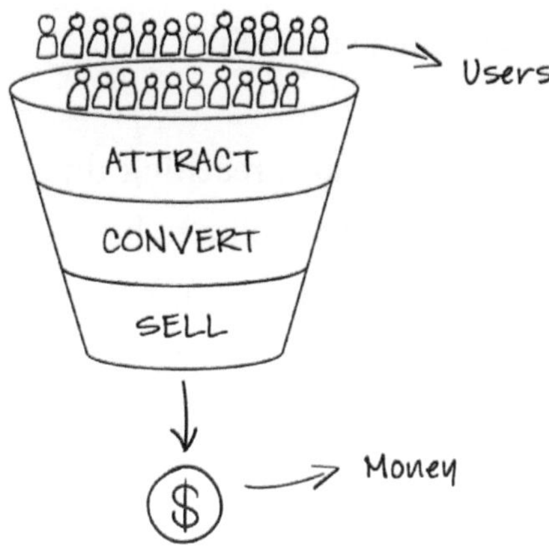

Minimum viable sales funnel.

Amazon takes care of all of these steps without you needing to do anything. And if you want to increase your sales or profits, it has its own marketing platform so you can add more users to the top part of this funnel.

8. You don't need to provide customer service.

Questions, delivery, refunds, complaints... Amazon will take care of it! All you have to worry about is making sure your account number is typed correctly so you can receive your royalties on time.

9. You can repeat the process again and again.

Does $1000 not even cover your mortgage? Then write a second book and double your income, or a third book and triple it, or a fourth... have I made my point?

Creating your first book and reaching this amount monthly may be a real challenge (you're going to have to break through a lot of mental barriers in the process), but once you've done it, you'll see it all from a different perspective and I'm sure you'll be spurred on to write the next one – this time, dedicating much less time to it.

10. It's a good *first step.*

Even if, like me, your dabbling in the online world goes beyond writing or earning $1000 a month, a book is a great starting point:

- It will enable you to create a real empire based on your work if you decide to use it as a means to position yourself as an expert **in your field** and attract customers to sell your products or services to.

- It will give you the confidence you need to tackle a new, more ambitious business **in another** field. When you see that it's possible to generate income without relying on a boss, your fears will be less likely to cause you to throw in the towel halfway and go back to the "security" of a traditional job.

And now that you know that freedom awaits you once you escape the system thanks to a single book...

It's time to sell your book!

CHAPTER 19

Bestseller in 24 hours

Have you ever been impressed by hearing that a friend or acquaintance was a bestselling author? Have you felt some healthy – or not so healthy – envy for that person? Did you think it was a feat only a select few with the gift of writing could ever hope to achieve? Did you think it was something you yourself could never manage?

I've got great news for you!

Not only can **you be a bestselling author on Amazon,** you can get there **in less than 24 hours!**

Yep, I'm telling you the truth. I promise. If I'm not, I'll invite you round for dinner.

So how do you do it?

This may surprise you, but Amazon recalculates the position of all the books on its platform **each hour and for each**

category. This means that, if your book *just happens* to be the most sold in a given category on a single day... **Amazon will give it a "bestseller" badge**.

Now we know that reaching bestselling position on Amazon depends on just two factors – your book's **categories** and its **sales in 24 hours** – you can prepare a launch strategy that guarantees you'll achieve this recognition.

Launch strategy

For this launch strategy, we will be focusing on the digital (Kindle) version of your book, for several reasons:

- It's better to focus your energies.
- The digital version allows you to use some good marketing tools and strategies.
- The physical version will benefit from the achievements of its digital brother, as both will appear linked on Amazon.

1. Put your book on preorder.

Approximately **one month before** the date on which you want to publish your book, I recommend putting it on preorder with KDP. This is as easy as checking a box and indicating your chosen publication date.

Pre-order

I am ready to release my book now

Make my Kindle eBook available for Pre-order. Is KDP Pre-order right for me?

Set Release Date (GMT)

01/25/2022

Although it's an optional step, doing it this way will enable you to benefit from the advantages of *Kindle Countdown Deals*, (as long as your launch is happening in a market that allows it).

2. Request your categories.

Within hours of putting your book on preorder, you will be assigned an ASIN number, which you can see from your KDP dashboard.

Once you have this number, you can request the categories for your book.

As I explained in the previous section, you need to do a little research to identify the categories with the best chance of raising you to bestseller status, and once you've published your book, write to Amazon to request that you be included in the best 10 of them (those with the highest ABSR).

3. Prepare your launch team.

Your *launch team* is basically going to consist of a group of family and friends who are prepared to buy your book within 48 hours of its launch[18]. Some of them will do it because they're interested in the topic and really want to read the book, others because they're proud to own a book you wrote, others simply to support you... It doesn't matter why they do it, but the bigger your launch team, the better. Of course, if you have followers or fans you want to add to this group, then go ahead.

Try to get at least 20 people on this team. The higher the number, the more positions you'll climb in Amazon's ranks, and the more effective your launch will be.

Becoming a bestseller in a subcategory is not the same as doing it in a main category. And, I repeat, this is going to depend on the sales you can obtain within 24 hours.

It's important to have your team prepared in advance, but don't go crazy, obviously; two or three weeks is more than enough. Explain as much of it to them as you think is necessary, but above all, don't forget to tell them their main mission will be to buy the book **on the day you ask them to**, that is, the first day of your launch.

---

[18] I recommend doing the launch around a week after your book is published, so you can take advantage of the boost Amazon gives new books in their first few days.

IMPORTANT: I'm sure a lot of people on your launch team will want to buy the physical version of your book so that you can sign it and they can put it on their favorite bookshelf where everyone can see it, but you need to make it clear to them that **their task is to buy the digital version**. If they want to buy both, then great – but first things first.

4. Select your marketing platforms.

In most markets, having a launch team of around twenty people is enough to reach the top position in one or more of the categories you've requested on Amazon. However, if your target market is Amazon.com, things are a little more difficult. This isn't a bad thing; it means that more (far more) books are sold in the US than in any other market, so if you do things right, you can earn more (far more) money. So, let's do things right.

Luckily for us, there are many platforms in the US that enable you to promote your book during its launch.

Using the services of one of these platforms is as simple as filling out the details of your book, choosing the day you want to promote it on, and paying the corresponding fee.

You'll encounter fees for everyone's budget: from free to prohibitive, such as over $500. Usually, the results you'll obtain will vary in accordance with the price you pay – but be careful! That's not always the case.

To avoid buying a pig in a poke and to be as safe as possible, I recommend choosing your platform from the exhaustive list compiled by *Reedsy*:

soykevinalbert.com/promo-platforms

For my US launches, I usually choose four or five platforms and try not to invest more than $170 in total.

To optimize my investment, rather than concentrating all my promotions on one day (something Amazon doesn't seem to favor), I configure each platform for a different day, making sure they coincide with my Kindle Countdown Deal.

For the first day of your Countdown Deal, you don't need to hire a promotion platform, as that's the day you'll be making good use of your launch team.

5. Configure your Kindle Countdown Deal.

As you will know if you read the second instalment of *Successful Self-Publishing*, this type of promotion enables you to sell your book at a discounted price for a limited period of time. Customers will be able to see its usual price alongside the promotional one on the book details page, as well as a clock showing the time remaining for the promotional price.

All you have to do is select a **start date** and an **end date** (with a maximum of seven days in between), the **number of price increases** (with a maximum of five) and the **starting price**.

In your case, I recommend setting your Countdown Deal for five to seven days (depending on the marketing platforms you decide to use) a week after your book's publication date, with a starting price of 99c and just one price increase. This means that your book will be available for 99c for the days you set the promotion for, and then return to its usual price.

IMPORTANT: In order to activate a Countdown Deal a week after publication, do not skip the first step – preorder – as your book must have been signed up to KDP Select for at least 30 days before starting your promotion.

Running a Countdown Deal during your launch serves two purposes:

1. **Increasing your sales**: both your organic sales, including those of your launch team, and those from the marketing platforms you decided to use. A discounted price along with the urgency created by the timer Amazon puts just above it will have immense power.

2. **Increasing your profits**: Unlike if you manually reduced your book to 99c instead of using a Kindle

Countdown Deal, your royalties will not be reduced to 30% but rather will stay at their usual 70%.

6. Launch your book.

It's time for your launch; day 1 of your Countdown Deal.

It's time to get your launch team into action.

You can contact them however you prefer: via WhatsApp, email, phone... What matters is that you ensure they get your message that same day, and that you notify everyone at the same time. Don't divide this task up and tell a few people in the morning, others in the afternoon, and others in the evening. Sit down and don't get up until you've finished the task.

C'est fini!

If you follow these simple steps, **I guarantee you will reach bestseller position** in one or more of the ten categories you requested.

Remember you can find out the number of books you need to sell in 24 hours in order to occupy the nº1 spot in any category by using *Publisher Rocket*[19].

---

[19] *soykevinalbert.com/rocket*

Checklist and timeline.

Given the importance of following these six steps in the correct order and at the right time, I have prepared for you a checklist and corresponding timeline.

One month before publication:

☐ 1. Put your book on preorder.

Three weeks before publication:

☐ 2. Request your categories.
☐ 3. Prepare your launch team.
☐ 4. Select your promotional platforms.

The week of publication:

☐ 5. Set up your Kindle Countdown Deal.

One week after publication:

☐ 6. Launch your book.

So, now that you're a bestseller, and before moving on to the next chapter, I have some bad news for you...

Being a bestseller won't do you any good.

During my research, I invested nearly $600 in a course that promised to teach us how to become Amazon bestsellers. I have to say that, although I ended up cursing the conman who sold me the course, it did deliver on its promise. That is to say that it taught exactly what I myself have just taught you in barely ten pages, but in video format and for around **100 times the price of this book** (and we've barely even begun).

It was my mistake, and I've observed that it's very common. Until recently, when I heard the word "bestseller", I associated it with sales (a lot of them) and money. However, the reality is different: become a bestseller on Amazon (without a good strategy behind you) does nothing more than inflate your ego and kid those naïve people who still think it equals success.

So, did I tell you this whole tale about how to become a bestselling author on Amazon just so that I could laugh at you, like the people who sold me that course? No.

Reaching this position, especially during your first few weeks after publication and with a strategy for afterward, is a fundamental step to succeeding in your work – which, in my view, consists of **selling a lot of books, getting a lot of income from them, and doing this over a sustained period of time**.

But don't be fooled – you don't achieve this by being a bestseller for a day. You need to be what is called a **longseller.**

CHAPTER 20

From bestseller to longseller

You can be a longseller without being a bestseller and vice versa, but I haven't taught you a strategy that guarantees you will reach bestseller position during your book's launch just to fill the pages up. As I said, **being a bestseller with a strategy for afterward** is a potent catalyst for the success of your book, because if you do things right, **it can generate sufficient momentum** to maintain sales in the long term. It is this – not getting that "best seller" badge – that I want to teach you with in this section: how to obtain a good passive income every month and make it last your whole life.

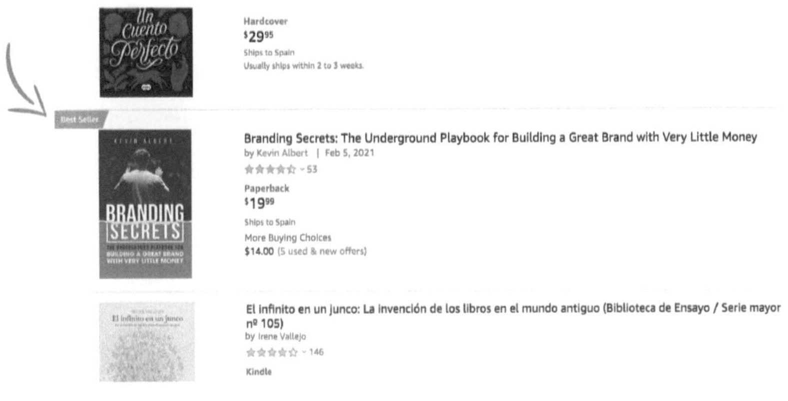

"Best seller" badge on search page.

It's important that you don't fall into the trap of thinking that if your book is a bestseller during its launch, your work here is done and you can just sit back and watch the sales keep rolling in. Let me insist one more time: this strategy is only useful for giving you the momentum you need to get started, but on its own it's not worth anything:

> I know a couple of gurus who, with their list of over 20,000 subscribers, performed a launch that not only enabled them to position their book as a bestseller in the best categories but actually reached nº 1 on all of Amazon... with a sh*tty book. The following week, it had dropped off the map, and the few genuine sales they were getting were receiving nothing but bad reviews complaining about the quality. It did these two gurus absolutely no good whatsoever to get their book as the top seller on all of Amazon, and just a few months later, they ended up pulling it.

> An even more noteworthy case is that of the *non-writer* Brent Underwood, an American marketing consultant who, with the sole aim of proving the worthlessness of becoming an Amazon bestseller, published a one-page book containing a picture of a foot entitled *Putting My Foot Down*[20] – and got it to be an Amazon bestseller in under five minutes.

---

[20] *soykevinalbert.com/pmfd*

I recommend that you google Underwood's story, but if you feel too lazy to do that then here are two extracts from interviews with him after his feat:

- «People get to the top of a category and, even if it only lasts an hour, they make sure they mention it in all their bios and they brag about it for the rest of their lives.»
- «There are all kinds of shameful websites promising secrets, tricks, conferences and online seminars for becoming a bestseller overnight.»

Now that you're clear on that reaching bestselling position is simply an intermediary step on your way to becoming a real longseller and increasing your income, let's move on to the next step.

The 7 keys to becoming a longseller

For your book to become a longseller, it's as "easy" as this: after its launch, it must continue to achieve a considerable number of sales. For this to happen, there are 3 requirements or stages: your book being shown (visibility), your book piquing people's interest, and your book selling.

Fortunately for you, with Amazon, you have the power to directly impact each of these 3 stages, bearing in mind 7 key points:

1. The title.

As we learned in the first section, no matter how good your book is, it's no use if readers can't find it.

Remember the formula for a perfect title:

FPT = keywords (SEO) + solution (sore point) + personality + time limit

2. The cover.

If the title is the main factor in helping readers find your book, then without a doubt the cover is the **main factor in capturing their interest**. A well-designed cover – designed for sale – will attract users' attention and get you more clicks than the competition.

In addition, if Amazon's algorithm detects that your book is getting more clicks, it will assume that it is relevant to readers and move it up the ranks, which will give it even more visibility.

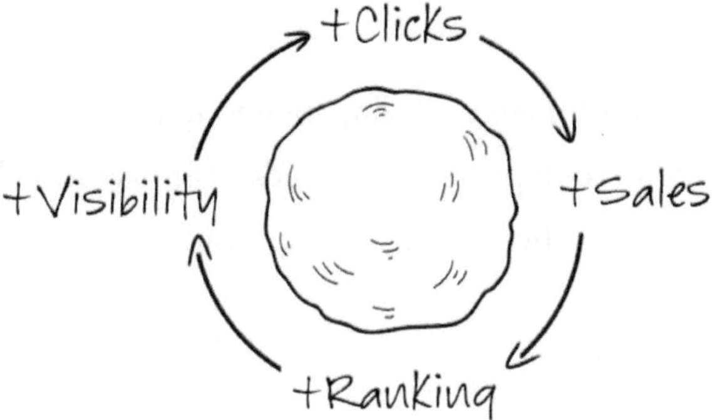

Snowball effect

Given that the cover will play such an important role in your book's success, you need to take it seriously.

Say it with me: **my book's cover must be designed by a professional**.

4. The description.

Once a user clicks on your book's icon in the search results or Amazon recommendations, they will be redirected to the product page: a page that Amazon has prepared solely for your book. There, the user can obtain absolutely all the information they need in order to decide whether to buy it. Among all this information, the element with the most persuasive power is, without a doubt, your book's description. A description written using persuasive language and presented in a format that your potential readers enjoy.

5. Look inside.

If your description isn't convincing enough to close the sale, the next element your prospective reader can use to help them make the decision is the "look inside" option.

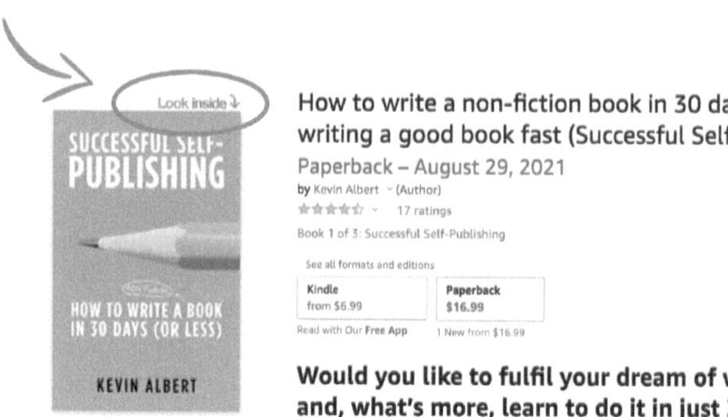

Location of the "look inside" option.

This feature is the digital equivalent of flicking through the pages of a book in a bookshop; it enables the reader to see the first few pages, 10%[21] to be precise, before deciding whether or not to buy it. Being aware of this will allow you to optimize your content in order to:

- Increase your percentage of sales.

- Get the email addresses of those who can't decide.

---

[21] You can write to KDP and request that this percentage is modified if you want.

Increase your percentage of sales

Managing to increase the number of users who end up buying your book after using the "look inside" feature is as simple as applying these two basic strategies:

1. **Take care over your contents page**. The contents page is the most-visited part of a non-fiction book, so in addition to creating it as early as possible, it's important that you take care to redact the chapters in an appealing way.

2. **Get straight to the heart of the matter**. After your contents page, get straight to the content. **Demonstrate as soon as you can that your book is worth reading**. It's important that you don't leave the best till last and that you don't repeat what you've already said in your description or add sections that Amazon already has specific places for, such as your bio, which goes on your author page.

Get the email addresses of those who can't decide

It's highly like that, if the user leaves your book's page without completing checkout, you've lost that sale forever. That's why it's a great idea to use these first few pages to get their email addresses by offering them something in return: a free resource, access to a private video relating to your book's topic, an invitation to a webinar[22], or similar.

Having the contact details of these undecided users means you can put into practice hundreds of strategies that will enable you to increase your profits to a point you're happy with. Although this is something on the level of a master's in digital marketing, the simple act of sending an email from time to time to your list of contacts and talking about some interesting topic relating to your book's subject **will improve your sales for minimal effort**.

6. Author's page.

In my time as a businessman, I learned (the difficult way) something I'll remember forever:

To get a sale, you need to sell not just the product but also your company and ***yourself****.*

The lack of any of these three elements will prevent the sale from taking place, especially when we're talking about products with a higher price.

On a platform like Amazon, we don't need to sell the company – we're already talking about the company with the best

[22] The term *webinar* is a neologism combining the words *web* and *seminar*. It refers to any content in video format whose main objective is educational and practical.

customer ratings in the world. So, if you do a good job selling your product via the correct application of the key components of this chapter, all that's left to do is **sell yourself** – and the right tool to do this with is your author page on Amazon.

The author page is the equivalent of the "about us" or "about me" section of a corporate website or personal blog. It's no coincidence that it's the page **most visited by users**: your customers need to know who you are.

You should use this section to forge a connection with your readers, generate trust, transmit professionalism... In short, to let people see the person behind the pages of the book(s) they are reading or thinking of reading.

Don't make the mistake of using your author page as a kind of resumé.

On certain occasions, mentioning your academic credentials may be advisable or even necessary – but the most important thing, and your main aim when filling out this section, is to empathize with your reader. If you can get them to identify with you and your story, they will be able to imagine themselves achieving the same things: the achievements you describe reaching with your book. If you can do this, the sale is guaranteed.

But be careful! Don't invent a backstory just because you think it will sell better. That's a short-term strategy that may end up biting you in the butt later.

> Many sellers of multilevel companies (such as Herbalife, to name one at random) hire cars and luxury houses just so they can take a selfie to post to their social media and grab a few foolhardy followers taken in by the so-called high life these conmen peddle by selling chocolate milkshakes. They are so cheesy that they even sometimes hire these luxuries in pools of several couples (for some reason, they love to show happy couples) and take turns to have their pictures taken.
>
> This type of lie may be somewhat useful for a period of time within the world of multilevel marketing or new infoproducers (they both use exactly the same strategies), but on Amazon you'll get caught out before you know it, and the house of cards will come tumbling down.
>
> Now that you know why this section is important and how to make the most of it, let's move on to the technical part.
>
> Unlike the other elements, your author page isn't filled in via your KDP dashboard. That's why many authors skip this step – whether out of laziness or obliviousness – which enables you to differentiate yourself and earn a lot of Brownie points in the eyes of Amazon and your readers.

The first step to creating your author page is to open an account with *Amazon Author Central*[23].

Once you've signed up, you'll find several sections at your disposal for turning your readers into your fans. That's right – as an author, you can have your own followers on Amazon.

Don't settle for just uploading your photo and bio: if you have a blog, don't hesitate to link to it, and if you have one or more videos where you present your book or talk about topics related to it, like a talk or conference you delivered, upload them! Let your readers see how you speak and express yourself – it will massively increase the degree of connection and trust they have in you. This is exactly what we want.

Note: if you upload a new book to Amazon having already created your author page, then for it to be shown on your profile you need to add it manually by going to the "Books" tab at the top and clicking "Add more books".

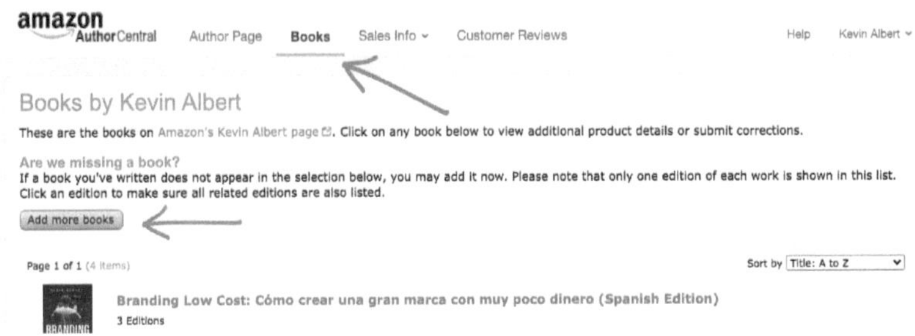

Location of "Add more books".

---

23 *authorcentral.amazon.com*

7. Your book itself (obviously).

Did you think that by applying a series of tricks and strategies, you could live off a crappy book? I have both good and bad news for you.

First, the bad news: that's not going to happen.

And now, the good news: I never get tired of saying that, unlike with fiction books, the success of a non-fiction book lies principally in whether it delivers on its promise. It may have spelling mistakes, be difficult to follow, read repetitively... but if the reader finishes your book having found the solution to the problem they were trying to resolve, you will have a satisfied reader.

I mean, do you really think that if I demonstrate with this book that it's possible to generate **a retirement pension in under a year** instead of in fifty years, anyone is going to be unhappy because I made a spelling error or because they don't like my jokes?

As you can see, in addition to having a good book, becoming a longselling author is as easy as...

- Getting found (**attracting**);
- Getting clicked on once you've been found (**converting**);
- Getting bought once you've been clicked on (**selling**).

In other words: you need to create a mini sales funnel where you have control over the effectiveness of each of its levels thanks to the 7 key points we just looked at:

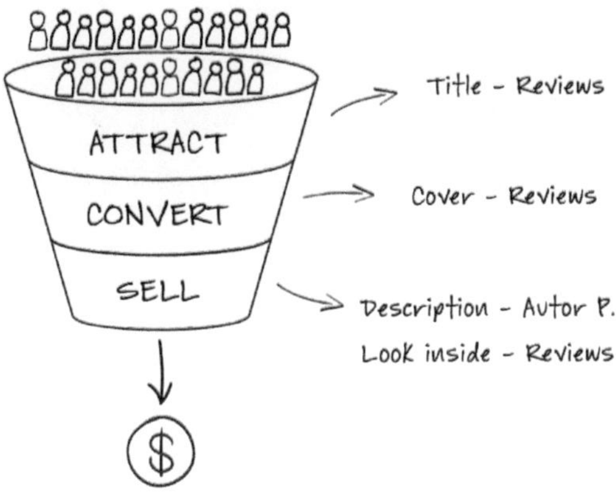

Main role of each of the 7 key points on each level.

As you can see in the image, although each element is interrelated, they each play a specific role on one of the three levels.

Did you notice there was one element repeated on every level and which I also "forgot" to mention in the list of 7 key points?

As I'm sure you can imagine, I didn't forget. The fact I saved it till last when I really should have made it the third thing I talked about – since it's the third element our potential reader will encounter – shows that it's so important when it comes to getting the sale that it merits its own chapter.

I'm talking about **Amazon reviews**.

CHAPTER 21

Reviews: the key to success

The reviews of a book carry a lot of the responsibility for an author's success or failure. And given that Amazon is the world leader in selling books, getting real reviews on the platform is essential.

Not many things hurt more than going through the difficult process of writing, publishing and launching a book just to see it achieve barely any sales and end up forgotten due to a lack of reviews.

Think about it: how many times have you bought a book without taking a look at the reviews? I don't know about you, but nowadays Amazon makes it so easy that I don't buy anything without reading a few comments from previous buyers or readers first.

Don't throw away all the work you dedicated to your book by missing out such an important aspect, because **getting the first reviews of your book is your responsibility.**

Why are they so important?

1. Credibility and social proof

When we search for a product, choose a restaurant, find a hotel to stay in or buy a book, we all look at the reviews and ratings.

A product with a lot of positive reviews on Amazon and an average rating of 4-5 stars gives us peace of mind when purchasing. We think that, if there are so many people satisfied with it, we probably won't be disappointed either. And in the case of a non-fiction book, **reviews tell us it really will fulfil its promise**.

This takes on extra importance when we're comparing two similar products. Imagine that one product had dozens – or hundreds – of positive 5-star reviews, while the other had none (or worse, had 1- to 3-star reviews), which would you pick?

A book with no reviews is not necessarily a bad book, but compared to a similar book with a large number of positive comments underneath it, the chances of the first being chosen by readers drop off drastically.

2. They influence Amazon's algorithm

Amazon, just like Google or YouTube, is a big search engine.

When people use it, the first results they see are determined by its internal algorithm, and reviews are an important part of this: they help you to improve your ranking.

The better your ranking, the more chance of people finding you – and the more chance of them finding you, the more likely you are to sell your book.

3. They drive sales

Each review you receive will improve your ranking, boost your credibility and attract potential readers who are more inclined to believe in the virtues of your book if they're mentioned by a third party (readers) than if you talk about them yourself.

On top of all this, there are several platforms – such as BookBub, Kindle Nation Daily and The Fussy Librarian – that will allow you to market your book for free once you reach a minimum number of reviews (between 5 and 10, with a rating of over 3.5-4 stars). This way, once you reach that threshold, you will have new opportunities to market (and sell) your book thanks to its reviews.

Warning: don't attempt trickery

Before explaining to you how to get these valuable Amazon reviews, it's important that you know **what you CAN'T do**.

Amazon has a zero-tolerance policy toward reviews designed to mislead or manipulate customers. Ignoring these rules may lead to the misleading review being simply deleted, or to your book being permanently removed from Amazon's catalog – or, worse, to your author profile being permanently closed with no recourse. And if you're living off your book, this is the equivalent of being fired from your company overnight with no appeal or redundancy pay, so BE CAREFUL.

Here is a list of the things you cannot doing when obtaining a review:

1. Pay or otherwise incentivize someone to leave a review.
2. Offer a gift for reviewing.
3. Offer a refund.
4. Swap reviews with other authors.

Finally, in the same way that misleading reviews in favor of your book are punished, bad reviews against books by your competition are also disallowed. Although there are still many "authors" (for want of a better word) who use this despicable technique, if Amazon or the author in question realize it's happening, the trickster may find themselves with a deleted account before they can blink.

Now that you know what you can't do, let's look at what's allowed in order to increase your book's reviews quickly and legitimately.

How to get reviews on Amazon

As a self-published author, having a good number of positive reviews on Amazon from the start can catapult your launch and make your work stand out above the competition.

That's why I want to highlight the importance of not considering publication complete until you've got these initial reviews. The more (real) positive reviews, the better, but **getting between 10 and 20 your first month after launching** is a good goal to aim for.

There are many strategies for finding readers prepared to leave a rating, but some take a lot of time... and money. There are platforms that sell them for around $200 each (complying with Amazon rules).

So, to get reviews during your book's launch or add them to a book you already published, we're going to look at **5 highly effective strategies** that won't require you to waste your money or your time.

1. Your launch team.

Having a good launch team will not only enable you to reach the top positions on Amazon when you publish your book, but it will also help consolidate you as a longselling author thanks to, among other things, the reviews this strategy can bring you in the first few days.

Generally speaking, getting half the members of your launch team to leave you a review is quite a feat. The main reasons some people might not do it include:

- They didn't like your book.
- They didn't read your book.
- They can't be bothered.
- They forget.

So, to try and ensure at least 50% reviews, and not to end up frustrated and annoyed, follow these steps:

1. **Don't send group messages/emails**: If you're going to ask someone to spend their time writing a review for your book, the least you can do is spend your time writing to or calling that person directly. Firstly, out of simple **courtesy and respect** (your time is no more valuable than theirs), and secondly because they will feel **more committed** if you write to them personally than if you

send a group WhatsApp, where they might think: "Out of all these people, they won't notice if I don't do it".

2. **Do an audit of your team**: Create a simple spreadsheet with the names of all your team members, so you can check:

    - If you notified them that your book was available for sale.
    - If they bought it.
    - If you asked them to leave a review.
    - If they left one.

    This way, you ensure no one escapes your notice and that you don't keep bugging those who already did their bit. Because, yes, you are going to have to bug people a little.

3. **Ask them to let you know**: Ask the members of your team to tell you once they've left their review, so that you can read it carefully. In addition to generating extra commitment, this will show them that you truly value their comments and that their opinion matters to you.

4. **They don't have to read the whole book**: One of the main reasons someone on your team might not leave you a review is that they haven't finished reading your book yet or even that they don't plan to read it at all, whether

because they don't have time or because they're not particularly interested in the topic. It's important to free them of this pressure by explaining that it's not necessary, that they can have an opinion on what they have read so far, and that if they want, they can modify their review later.

If you follow these steps, I promise that you will multiply the number of reviews you receive from your launch team.

2. Specialized Platforms: Booksprout and Book Bounty.

There are numerous platforms that facilitate the exchange of a free copy of your book for an honest review from the reader, all while complying with Amazon's guidelines. My two favorites are Booksprout and Book Bounty.

Booksprout:

Booksprout allows authors to distribute copies of their books to over 40,000 registered readers, offering options for both eBooks and audiobooks. The platform, which protects books from piracy, automates the sending of reminders and the tracking of reviews, significantly reducing the workload. It offers different subscription plans, from free options to premium plans with advanced tools.

Authors can request that readers/listeners leave their reviews on platforms such as Amazon, Goodreads, Audible, Barnes & Noble, Apple Books, Kobo, or Google Play Books.

If you want to try it for free for 30 days, use this link: www.soykevinalbert.com/booksprout

Book Bounty:

Book Bounty allows authors to obtain verified reviews through an exchange system. Authors read and review other authors' books, accumulating points that they can then use to receive reviews on their own books. The platform offers different subscription plans, from free options to paid plans with advanced features.

Unlike Booksprout, at the time of writing this, Book Bounty's reviews are directed exclusively to Amazon.

If you want to try it for free and also get a 15% discount in case you decide to subscribe afterward, use this link: www.soykevinalbert.com/book-bounty

Personally, I consider Booksprout an essential tool in any self-published author's toolbox. I use it not only to get reviews from new readers but also as my default means of sharing my books and audiobooks with my most loyal readers (my readers club). On one hand, it's much more professional to use this platform than to send a PDF or an MP3 via email. And on the other, it increases the chances that your book ends up in the hands of a genuinely interested reader, rather than someone whose only interest in your book is that it's free. You wouldn't believe the number of "readers" who, after asking you to share a book with them, decide not to download it just because of the extra step of doing it through Booksprout. It's a great way to filter your readers and separate your mailing list between "readers club" and "freeloaders club."

1. Ask for a review at the end of your book.

Not many readers realize just how important reviews are to us as authors. I'm sure that lots of people who enjoyed your book would be happy to leave a review if you just gave them a little nudge in the right direction.

And given that Amazon doesn't provide the email addresses or other contact details of our readers, we need to give them that nudge from within the book itself. Keep it concise and brief and remind readers to let you know what they thought. The best place to do this is in the last few pages, since good reviews tend to come from people who read the book all the way to the end.

Simply making this request will double the number of reviews you get. If you do it right, the proportion of comments left on each book read will go through the roof.

How to ask for a review?

A. Focus on giving.

There's nothing wrong with asking for a review, but if you want to get something, first you should offer something.

CAREFUL: I'm not talking about giving a gift in return for a review, as this is against Amazon's terms. I'm talking about having offered your readers a good book that entertained, excited, and inspired them... or, in the case of a non-fiction book, which **delivered on its promise**.

B. Emphasize the importance of their review.

In order for your reader to take the initiative, they need to understand that their review is important to:

- **Improve the book**: Explain that it will help you improve future editions of your book – or other books – if you can get their feedback.

- **Help other readers**: Emphasize the usefulness of a review to enable other readers to find your book and know what to expect from it.

C. Humanize your request.

Find a way to remind readers that there is a real person – not a big publishing company – behind the pages of your book, with real emotions and feelings. Tell them how hard the journey to finishing your book was, and how excited you are to be able to share it with others. By doing this, you can **get people to leave a review *for you*** as well as for your book.

Pro tip: As you know, a picture is a worth a thousand words, right? A quick and effective way to humanize yourself is to upload a non-professional picture of yourself in your request for a review. Show a side of your private life you think you readers could relate to or identify with: a family photo, a picture of your pet, you doing your favorite hobby (if this happens to be taxidermy, maybe go for the family photo instead...)

D. Just one request.

Many authors use the last few pages of their book to make all kinds of requests:

- Sign up to my newsletter.
- Follow me on social media (featuring seven links to their "main" socials).
- Buy my course or my other books.
- Hire my services.
- Leave me a review.

- ...

These are all good calls to action to end your book with, but if you don't want to overload your reader with so many requests that they don't end up doing any of them, **pick just one**.

Personally, I recommend that you always begin by requesting a review, and if once you reach a considerable number of reviews, you change it to your next favorite request. If you have more books, that one would be my second option.

Note: In the Kindle version, you can choose a different request from the start, since the system itself will suggest to the reader that they rate your book. This way, you will also avoid sounding repetitive.

E. Share the direct link to your reviews

Many authors, when asking for a review, include a link to their book's page in order to make the reader's task easier. Although this will go some way to increasing your conversion, it puts the onus on the reader to find the review page, and lots of well-intentioned people will throw in the towel before finding it and leaving their comments.

What if there were a way to include a link directly to the review page? All they would have to do is click and start typing.

There is, and it's really simple:

1. Depending on the format you want to direct your reader to – physical or digital – find the corresponding ASIN.

2. Add the chosen ASIN to the following link:

amazon.com/review/create-review?&asin=

Pro tip 1: Use a URL shortener. If you want your URL to look prettier (which will translate into higher conversion) you can use a URL shortener such as *Bitly*[24].

Pro tip 2: Create a QR code. Particularly for the physical version of your book, in addition to using a URL shortener, it might be worth converting it into a QR code[25]. Put yourself in the reader's shoes: imagine you're on the beach, reading a paperback, and the author suddenly suggests that you visit a website. What would be easier for you: to type a website address into your smartphone browser, or to go straight there by using your phone's camera?

4. Get your readers' email addresses.

As I mentioned above, Amazon does not provide any contact information for our readers (in my opinion, this is one of the

[24] *bitly.com*

[25] I use *codigos-qr.com*

biggest drawbacks to selling on this platform). This means that, unless a customer writes to us first, we have no way of getting in touch with them.

But **what if we could get our readers' email addresses?**

Well, first of all, having waited a reasonable length of time, we could write to them to ask what they thought of the book and **encouraging them to write a review**.

So, **how do you get them?**

Well, as always, by giving before expecting to receive. So, the first thing you need to do is think about what you can offer your readers that's sufficiently appealing – without going overboard – to convince them to give you their email address in return.

It could be access to an educational video or videos, attendance at one of your webinars, the audio version of your book, an Excel template, or similar.

Once you've decided what to offer your readers, you need to let them know that in order to access this free resource, all they have to do is drop you an email asking for it.

There are several ways of automatizing this process, but until you start receiving so many requests that it takes you more than an hour each week to reply to them, doing it this way will be enough. But if you do want to learn how to automatize the process from the start, drop me an email at books@soykevinalbert.com with the subject header *Automatization.* KIDDING ;)

Finally, **where should you put this message?**

It's easy. If you put your request for reviews at the end of your book, put your request for emails at the beginning, if you can, or at the end of the chapter that relates to the free resource you intend to offer.

Now that you have your customers' contact details, **use them responsibly**. Although the readers gave you their express permission to contact them, always try to follow this rule:

Only contact your readers if you have something to offer them.

In the first email you send, it's easy to use the excuse that you're interested in what they thought of the book and want to clear up any doubts they might have before asking them to leave a review. But if you don't get a review from them after this and you want to ask for one again, think carefully about what your second email will offer them before you write it. If you can't think of anything, I'm sorry, but you can't bother them again.

5. Relaunch your book

A great way to give your book's sales an extra push while getting a good number of fresh reviews is to do a relaunch.

This simply consists of **getting together a new launch team** and, if you want, including a new chapter or update (one that adds value, of course). This way, not only will you get those new reviews you want, but you will also climb back up Amazon's rankings, which in turn will attract more sales.

Note: This strategy is perfect for writers who want to revive a book they had already published on Amazon before they read this guide.

How to manage bad reviews

Receiving positive reviews is a real boost. For someone you don't know from Adam and who may be on the other side of the world to leave you a 5-star review on Amazon really makes you feel that all your hard work was worth it.

But, luckily or unluckily, sooner or later someone is going to give you a bad review. It's life, but don't worry – **it's not always a bad thing**:

1. **They show you're selling**. The best way to ensure you don't receive any bad reviews is not to sell a single copy of your

book. I'm sorry to tell you that, if you follow the steps in this guide, that's not going to happen. Authors who sell well or very well are going to get bad reviews, so unless you get more bad than good, BE HAPPY ABOUT THEM.

2. They give you credibility. A book with only positive reviews can sometimes seem not real. Having a negative review in there helps convince your potential readers that the other reviews are genuine.

3. They give you the chance to improve. Of course, if the review doesn't say much more than "your book sucks" or "I didn't like it", it's not awfully useful – but if you come across one explaining exactly what the reader didn't like, it gives you the chance to review that part of the book and improve or even remove it if you think that you should. Pay special attention to multiple comments mentioning the same thing.

Now that you've discovered the positive side of a negative review, let's look at how to handle it when they appear:

1. Keep perspective. I know, through my own experience and that of my clients, that your first impulse when you get a bad review is to get mad if you know your book is fantastic or to get depressed if you were already questioning your own work. Neither of these two states of mind will help you tackle the situation the way you should, so it's very important to keep perspective. Firstly, remember that a bad review isn't always a negative thing – as we just looked at – and secondly, I recommend that you think of your favorite book. Find it on Amazon and scroll to its reviews. Surprised? Who could have imagined that that amazing book that changed your life could have so many negative reviews underneath it? I bet that bad review that's been keeping you up at night doesn't seem so serious now.

2. Categorize your reviews. I advise you to try to include the review in each of the following 3 categories, as we will act differently depending on each one: constructive, useless or malicious.

- **Constructive: use these to improve**. As we have seen, if the review contains useful information and explains what drove the reader to leave a negative comment, you can use it to update and improve on future editions of your book.

- **Useless: ignore these**. If they do not give us any information but simply complain without making a point, the best thing you can do is to ignore it and keep doing what you do: sell books.

- **Malicious: report these to Amazon**. If a review is offensive or you notice something suspicious in it that makes you think that it was left by your competition with the sole aim of reducing your overall rating, you can report it to Amazon and request its deletion. To do this, all you have to do is click the "report abuse" button just below it.

Once you've reached this point, you have all the tools you need to guarantee that your book becomes a true longseller that will keep on selling without you needing to lift a finger.

Does this mean that you can just lay in a hammock and wait for those thousand monthly dollars to come rolling in?

Well... there may be situations where this happens (several of my students achieved this in their first month after launch, without needing to do anything else), but I'm sorry to tell you that this is usually more down to a stroke of luck than anything else, especially outside of the US market (where it does happen often).

The truth is that for the vast majority, **earnings will consist of around $170 to $350 a month**, and this is if you do things right and according to everything I've said so far: if not, your income will likely be much closer to $0 than to $170.

HOLD UP! That's not what you promised! I hear you say.

Calm down.

Although this is all you can expect to learn from other books, in the best-case scenario, with this book... **we're just getting started**.

CHAPTER 22

The DTP method: $1000 a month guaranteed

You may not know this, but this book originated in a *crowdfunding*[26] campaign on Kickstarter (if you're curious, you can take a look at it here: *soykevinalbert.com/kickstarter*).

Although it was a real success and I had no trouble reaching my funding goal, there were many people – writers included – who accused me both privately and publicly of being a liar and a scammer. This was because they believed that it wasn't possible to guarantee $1000 a month with just one book, especially in under a year.

[26] Crowdfunding is a collective funding model where various people from all over the world contribute small or large amounts to help make a project happen.

Real public comments during my crowdfunding campaign.

Among the authors who accused me of being a charlatan, there were **even some who acknowledged that they made $1000 a month** (or much more) from one of their books, but others where they barely broke $170.

This is a fact: some books will sell better than others.

To give you an example, an acquaintance of mine has several published books and, while most of them don't bring in $1000 a month, one in particular generates over $17,000 for him every month. He himself acknowledges that he doesn't know what's so special about that book, and attributes its success to luck.

Of course, this could happen to you too, and you could start earning not just 1000 but over 10,000 dollars right from the start, with barely any effort required. But just like this guy, it would be a matter of luck, and I can't help you with that. If what you're looking to do is hit the jackpot, you'd better stick to the lottery.

Where I can help you is by **guaranteeing $1000 a month**.

How is this possible? Didn't I just say in the previous chapter that earnings would usually hit around $170 and $350 a month? Am I running away with myself here?

Not at all – this is where MY METHOD comes into play. You can call it *The Kevin Method for Writers and Non-Writers of Non-Fiction Who Want to Live Off Their Books and Tell Their Bosses to Go to Hell...* or you could call it the DTP Method: Divide, Translate, Promote.

With this method, you'll keep leaving it up to fate whether you hit the jackpot and earn $10,000 or more from just one book without having to do anything, but you'll guarantee that $1000 a month by applying these three simple strategies.

Strategy nº 1: **divide**.

As I just explained, some of the authors who wrote to me during my crowdfunding campaign admitted that, although they made good money from some of their books, others didn't break $170. Through my own experience and that of my colleagues and clients, I can say it's rare for a book to give you less than that if you've done your job properly (the steps I've explained to you so far). However, we are going to be pessimistic just for a moment: let's imagine that, once you launch your book, you only make $100 a month.

I think that even those who wrote to me to call me a scammer and a liar would agree that **you can guarantee $100 a month**.

If you sell your book at $19.99, your royalties per book will come in at around $10[27]. This means that if you sell ten books, a month, you're already at $100. And bear in mind that, for reasons of simplicity, I'm not including the royalties from your book's digital version in this, and these will often be lower than for the physical version.

Do you think you can get ten measly sales a month from a bookstore (Amazon) that has over 300 million users? Easy, right?

Let's keep going!

---

[27] This will depend according to number of pages: the more pages, the lower the royalties (if the sale price is the same).

I'm sure that, in your first book, you tried to condense all the knowledge and experience you've accumulated over the years, and write a book to be proud of. That's commendable, and the sensation of self-realization is incomparable, but that doesn't mean that a fat tome with a gazillion chapters will sell more than a slim little book that focuses on just one of those chapters.

Did you know that books of between 5000 and 15,000 words are trending on Amazon, and that they are selling very, very well?

Readers – particularly of non-fiction – are searching more and more for books that get straight to the point, bringing solutions to their problems in a brief and concise way that can be consumed in a single sitting. So much so that Amazon has created a special category just for them: short reads.

I think you see where I'm going with this.

What if you were to divide your book into chapters – the most important ones – and publish them separately, as short reads or mini-books?

Imagine that, in addition to publishing your book, you publish another five mini-books made up of the five most important chapters from your first. The number of shorter books you can publish will depend in part on the length of the main one, of course, but I'm sure you won't find it hard to extract five good chapters that could work on their own.

With this simple strategy, you will have **multiplied the profits from your book by six**, when in reality... **they're the same book, just in instalments!**

- Main book = $100/month
- Mini-book 1 = $200 ($100/month x 2)
- Mini-book 2 = $300 ($100/month x 3)
- Mini-book 3 = $400 ($100/month x 4)
- Mini-book 4 = $500 ($100/month x 5)
- Mini-book 5 = $600 ($100/month x 6)

You may be wondering: can a mini-book be sold at the same price as the main one? Well, it can, but it's not the norm, nor do I recommend it. But can it sell as many copies as the main one? Of course – and with a reduced price, among other things, I promise you'll sell a lot more of them. Even with a lower price, the important thing is that your profits are ultimately the same from the shorter books as from the long one.

Example:

Main book .... 10 sales x $10 = $100
Mini-books .... 20 sales x $5 = $100

Can you think of a faster way to multiply your income from your book?

Think about it: even in the best-case scenario in which you apply my *Writer in 30 Days* method, writing a good book will involve several weeks of work. But **dividing it up will only take a few hours**.

Not convinced by the idea of chopping up your book? I understand – at first, I couldn't see it, either. I thought that it meant selling incomplete books, when it was really about selling **super-specific or specialized books,** and they were very well received by readers.

Once you change your perspective, a new world of possibilities will open up before your eyes.

7 hidden benefits of dividing up your book

1. It increases your authority.

If you think publishing a bestseller in your chosen field gives you authority, imagine what several under your personal brand can do for you. People will perceive you as more of an expert if you have ten published books than if you just have one, even though it's really the same thing!

2. Better reach and visibility.

When you divide your book into several miniature ones, you will have the chance to use specific keywords for each of them.

This, among other things, will enable you to try **as many different titles as mini-books** that you decide to publish, and as you now know, *a book's title is the nº 1 secret to getting discovered on Amazon.*

By doing this, you will be multiplying your chances of being found by your potential readers.

3. There's something for everyone.

You may think that if you write a book on a given topic, you are writing the perfect book for everyone interested in that subject. However, some people prefer to read a more specific book that focuses on a single point or idea.

By dividing up your book, you will be creating the perfect book for a higher number of people, increasing your sales.

4. There's something for every budget.

Although a book is a relatively low-cost item, there are people who find it hard to stump up, say, $29 for a tome that only contains one chapter that interests them – especially by an author they don't know yet.

Mini-books enable readers to pay less because they focus on just one point or chapter from the main book.

Since the investment needed is less, more readers will decide to give you a chance – and if they like what they read, they will be much more likely to end up buying the other mini-books in the series, especially if you put in a good introduction to the next one at the end of each of them.

You are offering readers the chance to buy your book in affordable instalments.

5. More income.

Let's say you decide to sell your main book for $19.99 (a relatively high price for a book, regardless of its length) and your mini-books for $9.99 each (a pretty low price, even for a short read).

If you divided your main book into five and a reader ends up buying them all – which is highly likely – then instead of making $19.99 on your main book, you will have made $49.95! Two and a half times more!

6. More lottery tickets.

I really don't like to rely on luck, especially when it comes to my finances. That's why I created this system where I guarantee at least $1000 a month for each book. But this doesn't mean that, if the gods of fate smile on one of my books and it starts generating $10,000 a month without me knowing how or why (just like what happened to my friend), I can start jumping up and down with joy. If I get that stroke of luck, then that's great, of course.

Well, by dividing your book up into several mini-books, you're effectively buying more "lottery tickets" and increasing your chances of your number coming up.

7. Motivation.

After the fact that **dividing your book will multiply your income,** this is my second favorite benefit when you're still in the process of writing your book.

Whether you're still finishing your book or you haven't started it yet, I recommend that you do the following: instead of writing it in full and then dividing it up and publishing, **start publishing the mini-books as you go along,** and then when you finish all of them, publish the main book.

I promise that seeing your mini-books start selling and generating income will give you the motivation you need to finish your book, and you won't end up like the millions of authors who start their books but never finish them.

I hope that with all the benefits – both to you and to your readers – that I've told you about, you're motivated to try this extraordinary strategy that will make things really easy for you when it comes to reaching your $1000 goal.

All that's left is to look at...

How to divide a book.

Once you change your way of thinking and start looking at mini-books as super-specialized books that have great value for readers by providing specific solutions to specific problems, you will be able to think of dozens of ways to divide up your book. You could create series of short readers from the sections of your main book, others from its chapters, or you may even realize that certain points you make are better expressed in individual books (that aren't part of a series) with just a small mention of those points in the main book, and so on.

To help make this clearer and hopefully inspire you, I'm going to show you the (provisional) division and publication plan for my main book: *Living Off Your Book.*

This was the initial contents page I intended to include:

1. WRITE YOUR BOOK
Chap. 1 – Why write a book?
Chap. 2 – Excuses and writer's block
Chap. 3 – What to write
Chap. 4 – The title
Chap. 5 – How to write your book
    5.1. The magic of mind maps
    5.2. The power of research
    5.3. The structure of your blueprint
Chap. 6 – Challenge: Writer in 30 Days

2. PUBLISH YOUR BOOK
Chap. 7 – Self-publishing vs publishing house
Chap. 8 – Editing
Chap. 9 – Layout
Chap. 10 – Cover
Chap. 11 – Description
Chap. 12 – Keywords
Chap. 13 – Categories
Chap. 14 – Pricing
Chap. 15 – Upload your book to Amazon

3. SELL YOUR BOOK
Chap. 16 – Bestseller in 24 hours
Chap. 17 – From bestseller to longseller
Chap. 18 – Reviews

Chap. 19 – Your retirement book
    19.1. Strategy nº 1: divide
    19. 2. Strategy nº 2: translate
    19. 3. Strategy nº 3: promote
Chap. 20 – Amazon Ads
Chap. 21 – Facebook Ads
Chap. 22 – Audiobook
Chap. 23 – Crowdfunding
Chap. 24 – Preorder on Amazon
Chap. 25 – Relaunch your book

How many mini-books could you get out of all this? So far, I plan to get 12 books from my original one. And I'm sure that many new ideas for mini-books will come up along the way:

1. Mini-book: *Write Your Book* ($4.99)
2. Mini-book: *Publish Your Book* ($4.99)
3. Mini-book: *Sell Your Book* ($6.99)
4. **Main book**: *Self-Publishing Secrets*[28] ($9.99)
5. Mini-book: *Audiobook* ($4.99)
6. Mini-book 4: *Amazon Ads* ($9.99)
7. Mini-book 5: *Facebook Ads* ($9.99)
8. Mini-book: *Crowdfunding* ($4.99)
9. Mini-book: *Relaunch Your Book* ($4.99)
10. Mini-book: *Cover* ($1.99)
11. Mini-book: *Editing* ($1.99)
12. Mini-book: *Layout* ($1.99)
13. Mini-book: *Reviews* ($1.99)

[28] The book you're reading right now.

I organized the list in the order in which I intend to publish the books, and indicated the price I intend to do it at (Kindle version).

Making a list like this in advance, with the possible division of your book into mini-books, can also ultimately give you a better version of the main one, since you won't feel the need to include absolutely everything in it purely to show how much you know or to avoid leaving anything out. Some chapters, no matter how interesting, are better as standalone books, so that you can improve understanding of them and increase the value of your main book.

Pro tip: Once you have made your list, take a look at **which mini-books could work as a series**. For example, I decided to group together 1, 2 and 3 from my list in the series *Successful Self-Publishing* (write, publish and sell). This way, when you upload them to KDP, you will be able to indicate that they are a series, and Amazon will notify readers who buy one of them that there are others in the series, which will obviously improve your sales.

Considerations when dividing up a book

A little recommend for if you decide to utilize this strategy and divide your book:

Treat your mini-books with the same care as you did your main book.

Dividing a book into five short reads will take you less than a tenth of the time it would take you to write five new books, but that doesn't mean it doesn't require some work.

If you dedicated a week to preparing a good cover for your main book, took care over creating a title (and subtitle) that would enamor Amazon and your readers, put together a launch team to help you climb the ranks and get your first reviews... **you should do exactly the same with your mini-books!**

Pro tip: Use the endings of your mini-books to introduce at least one other mini-book, and add a **universal direct link** to it. This is particularly effective when the book is part of a series.

Why do I say universal link?

Many people don't know that Amazon is actually made up of a total of fourteen different online stores (*.com*, *.es*, *.fr*, etc.). This means that, if you share a link to your book on *Amazon.co.uk*, the user will be sent to the British version of the platform, and if they don't have an account there, they won't be able to buy directly.

Enter universal links.

Rather than ignoring your international readers or sharing fourteen separate links for each of Amazon's stores, you're going to create a magic link that will redirect users to your book's page in their country.

To do this, we are going to use the tool Booklinker. It couldn't be easier to use:

1. Go to *booklinker.com*.
2. Enter the URL of your book.
3. Click «Create Universal Link».
4. Personalize your universal link (with your book's title, for example).
5. Sign up.
6. That's it!

This is how the universal direct link to one of my books looks:

- **Before**: *amazon.com/gp/product/B08R73RXT3/*
  **Valid only for Amazon.es.*

- **After**: *mybook.to/branding-secrets/*
  **Valid for all of Amazon's fourteen online stores.*

Strategy nº 2: **translate**.

If you did a quick mental calculation in the previous chapter of the royalties my book would generate once divided into twelve parts, you will have realized that – without my doing anything else, and even with profits of $100 per month per book, which is a highly conservative estimate – I would reach and surpass my monthly goal of $1000.

But what happens if, despite trying your best to figure it out, you find that only four – not twelve – of your book's chapters warrant publication as individual books? We would be looking at "just" $500 a month. How do we get to the $1000 a month I promised you?

If you have already reached $500 a month by dividing up your book, and you don't want to (or can't find a way to) divide it up any further, what you need to do is as simple as **translating your book into another language... and DOUBLING YOUR INCOME**.

It may seem silly because it sounds so obvious, but do you know how many authors are achieving good book sales and still haven't had them translated?

I understand that someone who has published a book and scarcely made peanuts from it will have no intention of translating it to another language just so the same thing can happen again. But I can only think of two reasons why those authors who *are* obtaining good royalties from their books might not have them translated: they don't know how to do it, or they think it's too expensive.

If this sounds like you, we're going to look at two ways of translating your books into any language, simply and even for free!

1. Upwork: my choice.

Of all the places where you can look for a translator for your book, I once again recommend opting for *Upwork* and repeating the same steps you followed for the editing and layout of your book.

As with these tasks, prices vary hugely, and it's not unusual to receive quotes higher than $5000[29] but don't worry – by searching properly, you'll find good professionals to translate your book for under $100 per 10,000 words.

2. Babelcube: free.

Babelcube is a platform that puts writers in touch with translators. The former gets their book translated for free, and the latter take home a portion of the book's sales.

---

[29] Official prices (recommended by the Editorial Freelancers Association) for translating a book are between $0.09 and $0.19 per word.

Once you've reached an agreement with a translator and the work is done, Babelcube will publish your translated book on over 300 sales channels: Amazon, Apple, Barnes & Noble...

The system for sharing royalties varies depending on the number of units sold. The more sales, the better the conditions for the author: from 30% at the start, up to 75% once $8000 has been reached.

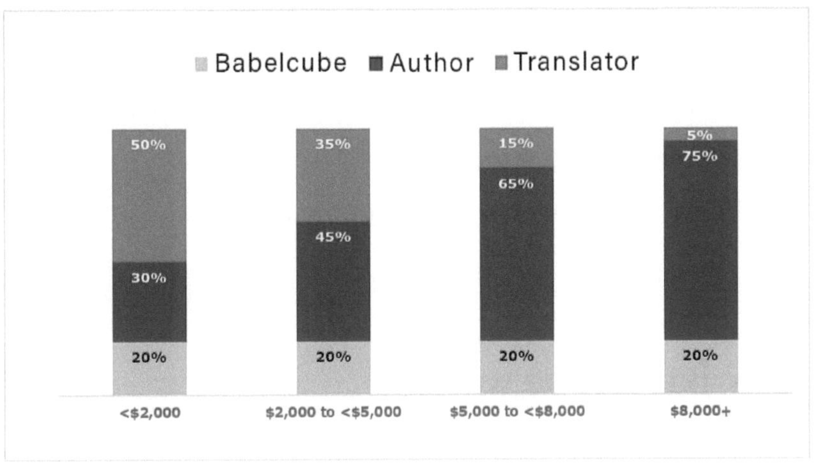

Distribution of royalties with Babelcube.

Something to bear in mind:

- Shorter books have more chance of getting a translator interested in them (since they involve less of a gamble).
- If you've had good results with your book in English, more translators will be willing to translate it.

- If no one is interested in your book when you upload it to the platform, you can contact translators directly. Babelcube offers a detailed list of its freelancers.

Advantages of Babelcube:

- Cost = $0 (you just share your earnings).
- The chance to translate your book into more than 15 languages.
- You choose your translator or team of translators.
- Sell your book on hundreds of sales channels and subscription services.
- Earn additional income in new markets.

How Babelcube works

1. Create an account. Provide as much detail as you can, as this will allow translators to get to know you. This will be your covering letter.

2. Create your book's profile. Post a profile for each book you want to have translated. Make sure you include all the information about its potential: sales history and royalties, reviews, awards and recognition (categories it has become a bestseller in) and any other information you think is relevant. It's also recommended that you include

a brief extract (maximum 2000 characters) from your book, so translators can provide you with a sample translation.

3. Choose your translator. Once you have uploaded your book's profile, you will start getting offers from various translators. Often, they work in teams: one will translate, while another edits and proofreads (what a luxury). For every proposal, they will indicate the target language and estimated timeframe. All you have to do is review the proposals, research the translators' profiles, and accept the offer from your chosen translator(s).

4. Check the translation of the first few pages. When the first ten pages have been translated, you will have an opportunity to check its quality, and if it's not good, you can cancel the job without being penalized.

   Pro tip: If you don't have the necessary level of the target language to be able to check the translation (which is normal) and you don't have any friends who can give you a hand with this, you may want to create a mini-job on Upwork for around $10-15 so that another freelancer can check the sample for you.

5. Review the final translation. Once the translation is complete, you can check it and suggest changes or

modifications before approving it. If for any reason you consider that the quality is insufficient, and you can't come to an agreement with the translator, you can cancel the job but you will be charged a fee.

6. Prepare your book for distribution. Babelcube will allow you to convert your book into various formats, publish it and edit it on its different sales channels.

7. Receive your royalties. Babelcube will pay you your royalties regularly, and you can track sales and payments from your user dashboard.

Now that you know two low-cost methods for professionally translating your book, I'm sure you will have already done the math: if dividing your book into five can net you at least $500 monthly, then translating it into even just one other language will get you to the goal I set with this book: $1000 a month.

So why not translate it into more than one language?

Of course, if for any reason you have your book translated and still don't reach $500 a month (although this would be unusual), I suggest you choose another language and repeat the process. Even better, if you have reached (or thrashed) that goal, you should still **choose another language... AND DOUBLE YOUR INCOME AGAIN!**

Strategy n° 3: **promote**.

I'm sure by now you've realized that just by applying the first two strategies of the DTP method, you can pretty much keep increasing your royalties as much as you want – but before you hang that medal around your neck and consider your goal reached, let me tell you about one final strategy that can help you to increase your passive income even more. This time, it won't come from your book's profits.

As I've told you, to find a system that enabled me to guarantee my retirement fund with just one book, I invested quite a lot of money (nearly $6000) in several training courses. Among them, I bought over $1000 worth of Facebook Ads. The creator, a well-known Spanish-language guru, personally promised me that **with Facebook ads, I could earn as much as I wanted through selling my book**. I was already pretty suspicious due to other, similar courses that had caught me out before, but since the guru and I had some mutual friends – and he was offering a double refund guarantee – I eventually decided to pay for the course. As you can probably imagine, it ended up not working, and despite his double guarantee I never did get my money back.

The reason why this course was not useful for making money from a book was that, like so many other courses, it was based on what is known in marketing circles as a **value ladder**, and to make use of this strategy you need at least one *hook* (or entry-level) product and one *premium* product or service:

1. **Hook**: you offer a product at a very low price (less than $20) or even for free. Its aim is to get customers' email addresses. Usually, spending on ads to bring users to the website where they can buy or download this product will be greater than the profit made from it.

2. **Premium product**: this has a higher price ($100 and up). It is offered to users who have bought the hook product. Statistics tell us that a percentage of these customers will also buy the premium product. This is where you get your investment back on selling the entry-level product, and where profit is made.

Do you see where the problem is in this system if you're trying to make money from just one book?

- **You have to pay to sell**. Your book is considered to be the hook.
- **It assumes you have a premium product to sell**. I didn't.

That is exactly why I requested – unsuccessfully – for my money to be refunded from the Facebook Ads course: I didn't want to have to pay people to read my book, nor did I have the time or the inclination to create a premium product right then, and I'm guessing, since you're reading this book, that you're in the same boat.

But what would you say if I told you that I ended up finding a way to create a value ladder without needing to invest money in getting your book read and which you could use to sell a premium product without needing to create one?

Sounds too good to be true? Remember that in your review ;)

1. How to sell your book without investing in ads.

This part is easy – I talked about it at the beginning of this section. Given that you're going to sell your book on Amazon and not via your own website, you don't need to spend money on marketing to attract potential readers – Amazon will take care of that!

2. How to sell a premium product without needing to create one.

Now for the good part. Instead of creating a premium product, **you're going to sell someone else's** :)

This way, it won't be necessary for you to design an extraordinary product that people are prepared to dig deep for. All you have to do is find that extraordinary product and promote it… in your book itself.

You might be wondering how the hell you're supposed to make money by promoting someone else's product. Let me give you a brief introduction to **affiliate marketing**.

Affiliate marketing is a system whereby an affiliate (you) promotes the product of a person or company (the producer) in exchange for commission on every sale.

It's a fantastic commercial system where everyone's a winner:

- **The affiliate**: they can monetize their website, social media, **book**... by selling third party products without doing the work involved in creating a premium product.

- **The producer**: they get new sales without having to invest in ads.

- **The customer**: they get more channels for finding information on products, and can make better purchasing decisions. The recommendation usually comes from someone they trust (you).

What product should you promote?

Before explaining the process of becoming an affiliate, first things first: what kind of product should you promote, and where can you find it?

Although on your value ladder, the premium product wasn't created by you, you need to apply the same logic we would use if you had done. The product you promote **should be an added**

or complementary step to your book. It would also be good to use a product with similar content but in another format (a video course, for example).

Taking my own book for example, I can think of a lot of products that might be of interest to people who read it: *How to Sell Your Services Using Your Book, Create a Course From Your Book, Facebook Ads For Authors, Amazon Ads For Authors, Crowdfunding For Authors, Write Your Book in 30 Days, Boost Your Personal Brand Through Your Book,...* Okay, so the titles need some work, but you get the idea, right?

I recommend that you make a list of possible courses or products that could align with your book before you begin your research.

Now that you have a few ideas for interesting products that might complement your book, it's time to find out if anyone else has already had those ideas and created courses out of them.

If you know enough about a topic to have written a book on it, I'm sure you already know the leading experts in your field and the best infoproducts on the market.

If, for some reason, you don't, you have two options:

- **Google it**. All you have to do is type in the names of the products on your list and the word "course". When you find what you're looking for, you need to find out if you can sell that product as an affiliate. I recommend that you email the course creator and ask them directly. The affiliate option is not always publicly advertised.

- **Search on** *Hotmart*[30]. This platform enables you to easily search through its thousands of products and filter them according to various criteria (sales commission, price, etc.). The good thing about searching on Hotmart is that, if you find a product that fits, it almost definitely has an affiliate option.

IMPORTANT: before you recommend one of these courses, you need to be sure of its quality and that it is worth what it costs. The best thing to do is recommend one you have tried yourself and liked. If you haven't done this, you have several options: buy it and do it, ask the expert to give you access to it for a few days to check it in depth, and/or research what other customers thought. Remember you're staking your reputation and credibility on this.

If you've written a book to be proud of, don't throw your work down the drain by recommending a bad or mediocre course just to earn a few extra bucks. Even though the course isn't yours, if you're the one who recommends it in your book, your readers will end up associating it with you and what they think of the course will affect what they think of your book.

---

[30] Hotmart is a platform specializing in the commercialization and distribution of digital products.

It needs to be a product that you would recommend even if you weren't earning commission on doing so: when you do this, you need to be adding value. For example, it would have cost me nothing to include an affiliate link to the Facebook Ads course I mentioned and earn around $600 for every reader who ended up buying it, but that would be unethical on my part, given that I wasn't satisfied with it myself.

How to become an affiliate

Being an affiliate of a course or product is as easy as having a personalized affiliate URL. Example:

- Normal URL: *supercurso.com*
- Affiliate URL: *supercurso.com/kevinalbert*

Both URLs lead to the same website – the user will see exactly the same thing. The only difference is that if a user ends up buying something on the website having followed the affiliate link, the affiliate will receive commission on that sale.

To get your affiliate link, all you have to do is sign up on the platform linked to the course you have decided to promote. Once you've signed up, you will be assigned an affiliate link and gain access to a control panel where you can track your sales.

Now that you have your affiliate URL, all you have to do is share it as is, or turn it into a QR code, like we looked at in the previous chapter.

Earning some extra money has never been easier.

Where should you put your affiliate link?

Given that the product you're going to promote should be a step on from your book, it makes sense for your recommendation and affiliate link to go at the end of the book. It's not just about logic – by putting it in the last few pages, you will also have more time to generate the trust you need from your reader so that your recommendation has more of an effect and a greater chance of conversion.

Be careful you don't go overboard with your final recommendation and end up making your book sound like a sales letter for the product you're promoting. Some people write books purely as tools for selling their course or someone else's. When this happens, it's obvious. Readers aren't stupid, and their dissatisfaction will be reflected in their reviews.

Your job is to recommend a product that complements your book or goes one step further. The onus of convincing a customer to buy the premium product lies with the product's creator.

Rather than using your book itself to talk about how amazing the course you're promoting is, what you can do is find a product that has a good sales page – or, even better, get an affiliate link that redirects to a webinar subscription. The conversion percentages for webinars are much higher:

- Affiliate URL> Sales page > Purchasing decision > **1-2% conversion.**

- Affiliate URL> Webinar subscription > Webinar > Sales page > Purchasing decision > **5-10% conversion.**

How much can you earn?

Now that you've chosen the perfect premium product that you want to promote, and you've included the affiliate link in your book, let's look at the numbers.

In order to get a rough estimate of the monthly commission you can earn as an affiliate, you need to know 4 things:

- **Product price**. Let's imagine the premium product you've decided to promote with your book costs $1000 (you can easily find infoproducts costing up to five times this much).

- **Commission per sale**. Out of this $1000, you take 50% - that is, $500 (50-50 is pretty normal for digital products, since they have no manufacturing costs and are pure profit).

- **Conversion percentage**. A good sales letter (your book) in the hands of a potential customer (your reader) will normally have around 2-4% conversion. This means that for every 100 books you sell, you should get around 2-4 sales[31].

- **Monthly sales of your book**. If we continue with the same numbers as above and say that, in addition to your main book (five sales per month) you have also published five mini-books on top of that (ten sales a month each), you will have a total of 55 sales a month. With these numbers, you would sell between 1 and 2 premium products every month, **adding $500-1000 in affiliate commissions to the monthly royalties you get from your book**.

So, what if you have your book translated into other languages, too?

Well, then you'd be able to **multiply those affiliate commissions by the number of languages your book comes in**. That said, you would need to do some careful research into a good premium product for each of these languages.

---

[31] If the product is cheaper, you'll be more likely to get a sale (and vice versa).

Tip: you can create a job post on Upwork for around $10-20 to help you find a good premium product in the language you need.

CONCLUSIONS

I hope that having read through the three strategies that make up the DTP method, those $1000 that you found dubious at the start of this book now seem easily achievable (easy peasy, even).

You see now that simply by dividing your book into four more mini-books, and translating them into other languages, you can reach your goal. You can also add your affiliate link to a premium product, create even more divisions, translate them into even more languages. If you do the math, you'll see that reaching $3-5000 a month from just one book is not at all unrealistic. So...

Why did I limit myself to guaranteeing $1000 a month?

Firstly, because that was the initial goal that drove me to write this book: to equal, in just a year, the retirement pension that it took my father more than fifty years to reach.

And secondly, because I have realized that when someone discovers the true potential of a book, the DTP method takes a back burner. Why carry on dividing, translating and promoting if you've already hugely surpassed your initial goal?

Can I tell you a secret?

None of my students has managed to divide their book into more than three parts or translate it into more than one other language, and yet they have ALL reached and surpassed their goal in under a year – some even during their first month.

How is this possible?

I like to explain it with what I call *the law of the corridor*:

Imagine you're standing at the start of a long corridor, with a big door at the other end. That door would be the goal you have set yourself (let's say, $1000 monthly from your book). Given that you can see your objective – the door at the end of the corridor – you start walking toward it. But along the way, you realize that there are other doors to the side that you would never have seen if you hadn't started walking toward the door at the end. Now for the good part: since you're curious, you decide to open some of these doors (the ones that most catch your eye) and behind them you discover new or better ways to reach your goal, or ways to surpass your original objective, showing you new goals that you would never have thought of but that make you completely forget about your initial goal once you know about them.

This law, applied to the objective of this book, could translate into your book and mini-books not giving you 50 but rather 500 each, your main book reaching those $1000 monthly out of nowhere, a publishing house contacting you and offering to pay you much more than you had planned for, getting your dream job thanks to your book, Amazon offering to turn your book into an audiobook and pay you handsomely for it, deciding to create your own premium product, and so on[32]...

If, as I say, this is always (or nearly always) going to happen, why did I tell you about the DTP method?

Well, because this method is going to be responsible for you beginning to walk toward that door at the end of the corridor. Most people aren't capable of taking even that first step if they can't see the way ahead clearly and know (or think) that there is no chance they'll fail. It's human nature. With my method, I've given you the confidence that no matter what happens, even if you don't find any more doors as you walk down the corridor, or even if you don't like what's behind them, your main objective is guaranteed.

---

[32] All of these are real examples from clients or colleagues of mine.

So, what's next?

First of all...

CONGRATULATIONS!

If you're reading this book for the first time and you still need to get to work, congratulations! Out of all the people who talk about writing a book, you form part of that little 1% who actually do something about it and decide to educate and inform themselves in order to fulfil their dream.

And, of course, if you've already written, published and/or achieved your first $1000/month with your book, CONGRATULATIONS! You can now proudly say you are officially a writer.

This is a truly a milestone in your life, and one worth toasting.

To sum up, in this book you have learned:

- How to overcome writer's block.
- How to find the perfect idea for your book, even if you thought you already had it.

- How to create the perfect title: one that Amazon loves and which sends your sales through the roof.
- How to write your book in 30 days.
- How to edit your book on a budget.
- How to get your book's layout as good as, or better than, a publishing house would.
- How to design and validate your book's cover from over a hundred different proposals.
- How to boost your book's sales thanks to good keyword searching.
- How to escape the rat race thanks to your book.
- How to turn your book into a bestseller in under 24 hours.
- How to turn your bestseller into a longseller that keeps on selling beyond its launch.
- How to get continuous, legitimate Amazon reviews.
- How to guarantee an income of $1000/month with the sales from just one book.
- How to start obtaining income from your book before you've even finished it.
- How to translate your book for free.
- How to sell a premium product without needing to create one.
- ...

So, now what?

Once you've reached at least $1000 a month with your book, the possibilities are endless:

- You can turn it into an audiobook and publish it on Audible.
- You can learn Amazon marketing and boost your sales and income.
- You can hire a ghostwriter to help you write your next books.... or, even better, to write them for you.
- You can train up in Facebook Ads and create a sales funnel from your own website
- You can create your own premium product and promote it in your books.
- You can, of course, write another book.
- ...

The journey you've begun doesn't end here. This is just the beginning of a great adventure. Becoming a writer isn't just a goal achieved; it's a door to a universe of opportunities. Every book you write, every idea you put on paper, not only brings you closer to your dreams but also has the power to touch lives, inspire others, and change the world.

Remember, success isn't measured only by sales figures or monthly income. True success is the satisfaction of having shared your voice with the world, of leaving a mark, of inspiring others to pursue their own dreams.

Keep writing, keep exploring, keep dreaming. The world needs more stories, more ideas, more authentic voices. It needs you. It needs your voice.

Thank you for allowing me to accompany you on this journey. I'm excited to see where your path will take you.

Hugs to you, fellow author!
Kevin Albert

My father (the reason this book exists) and me.

Important

In order for my book to help other readers like you, **your opinion is very important**. I would appreciate it greatly if you could **leave me a review** on your favorite platform to tell me what you thought of my book so that I can keep on improving it:

- What did you like the most?
- Is there anything you felt was missing?
- Is there anything you would add or remove?
- ...

A gift just for you!

Would you like to **read my next book completely FREE**? Scan the code below and **join my readers' club**!

Great surprises await you: be the first to read my new releases, listen to my audiobooks for free, get signed and personalized copies... and so much more!

Other books by Kevin Albert

www.ingramcontent.com/pod-product-compliance
Ingram Content Group UK Ltd.
Pitfield, Milton Keynes, MK11 3LW, UK
UKHW041635190726
13854UKWH00006B/2507